D0119596

1/-
5p

DISCUSSION BOOKS

General Editors:
Richard Wilson, D.Litt., and A. J. J. Ratcliff, M.A.

◊

WHAT ABOUT INDIA?

No. 4

WHAT ABOUT INDIA?

by

L. F. RUSHBROOK WILLIAMS, C.B.E.

*Quondam Fellow of All Souls College: Formerly Professor of
Modern Indian History in the University of Allahabad*

THOMAS NELSON AND SONS LTD
LONDON EDINBURGH PARIS MELBOURNE
TORONTO AND NEW YORK

First published, September 1938
Reprinted, February 1939

CONTENTS

INTRODUCTION

LAST summer I attended a meeting of a small club which assembles at irregular intervals to discuss present-day affairs. It cannot meet frequently because its members, mostly writers who study political problems and administrators who have to deal with them, are scattered over the four quarters of the earth, and do not often find themselves in London. At this particular meeting we were discussing the relations between East and West in their bearing upon the future of the British Commonwealth. Certain members, recently returned from the Far East, considered that the solution of this problem lay in the promotion of a better understanding between Britain and Japan. I ventured to urge that this was in reality a side-issue, however great its political importance at the moment : and that the real problem centred round the relations between the British and the Indian peoples. I urged that if India remains inside the British Commonwealth, as a free agent and by its own choice, as do the self-governing Dominions, it will constitute a bridge between West and East across which men's minds may move to a truer comradeship and a better understanding. After some discussion, many of my fellow-members thought that I had good grounds for my point of view ; but they doubted whether India would ever " fit in " to the Commonwealth.

This little book, which is intended to give people in

England some " background " for the Indian news they
read in the Press, will, I think, set out the difficulties
which were present to the minds of my critics ; but I
hope it will also explain why I think that India *can*
" fit in " to the free fellowship of the Commonwealth
of Nations if it wants—and if we help it to want—to do
so. But it is beyond my scope to deal with the larger
question of what India's willing adhesion to the Commonwealth will mean to the world. No doubt readers
will think this out for themselves.

WHAT ABOUT INDIA?

CHAPTER I

THE TEXTURE OF INDIAN LIFE

THE first thing to realize about India is that it is the home of an ancient, but still vital, civilization, which differs greatly from the civilization of the West. The ancient civilization of Egypt exists only for archæologists ; that of Sumeria must be uncovered by the excavators. But the civilization of India, in its origins probably as ancient as either, still exists in full flower before our eyes ; and is the greatest factor in the lives of people who to-day probably number three hundred and fifty millions, one-fifth of the entire population of the world. Perhaps it would be no exaggeration to say that this civilization *is* India ; because it provides the common basis which gives the whole country a fundamental unity. Without it India would be just a sub-continent, the size of Europe without Russia, broken up into a number of different countries inhabited by different races speaking different languages.

The peoples, races, and languages, very distinctly marked off one from another, do, in fact, visibly exist ; and for this reason some observers have maintained that India is a mere geographical expression ; that there are

Bengalis, and Rajputs, and Punjabis, and Gujaratis, and Marathas, and Sikhs, and Parsis, and Muslims, and Christians, and many other peoples, but no Indians—in fact, that there is no such thing as India at all. But this view is not much pressed now, if only because political events during the last quarter of a century have made it increasingly plain that even if the different peoples of India do not always see eye to eye on every issue, they possess quite sufficient consciousness of common unity to realize that they are very different from us, and to show that they are increasingly reluctant to allow us to control the destinies of their country. Much more will be said about this when we come to study the rise of the modern nationalist movement : it is sufficient here to notice that the whole basis of this movement is the consciousness among many of the Indian peoples that they have a common culture which sharply distinguishes them from the peoples of the West, and particularly from that Western people whom they know most about, ourselves.

The most typical thing about a culture is the outlook on life to which it leads : for eventually it is our outlook on life which determines what we are, whether as individuals or as nations. The Western nations of Europe and America, although they may differ in their political ideas, share one fundamental point of view, originally derived from the Greek Sophists, that " man is the measure of all things " ; in other words, that man stands, as it were, apart from the rest of creation ; can master natural forces ; can bring everything to the test of reason ; and approaches more nearly to perfection than other creatures. These ideas have been powerfully reinforced by the Jewish and Christian conception (which is also shared by Islam) of a personal God, whose care extends to every individual human being ; with the result that the individual is regarded as being of extreme importance, and human life is looked upon as of high value. Even in Communist or Totalitarian states, where there has been a reaction against individualism, man is regarded as the master, potentially at least, of the universe. And even where the existence of a Divine Being is denied, as in Soviet Russia, it is man's own achievements in the shape of machinery and a mechanical civilization that become the objects of worship.

What may be called the typically Indian viewpoint is quite different. According to this, man is merely part of a great universe, which is governed by impersonal cosmic laws to which even the gods themselves are subject. Thus man enjoys no outstanding predominance. Every created thing, mankind included, is in a perpetual process of dynamic change. Behind and beyond lie eternal Matter and eternal Spirit, from which everything in creation, from the great gods to the merest atoms, are temporary and always-evolving manifestations. These manifestations are alike in value, since they are all derived from primal Matter and Spirit ; are all subject to the cosmic laws ; and are thus all equally necessary for the functioning of the universe. The lives of gods, of men, of beasts, of plants, of stones, are all transitory ; and are just phases in a recurring cycle of births and rebirths. Each separate life has its task to fulfil in the great whole, and with this task go both rights and duties. The human individual is not singled out for any particular importance. Whether he is a prince or a pauper, his existence here and now is merely a transient manifestation of eternal forces ; and his life on earth is of small significance except as a link between his infinitely numerous lives in the past and his infinitely numerous lives in the future. Moreover, he is always a part of some larger whole ; of the celestial universe ; of the lesser terrestrial universe ; of human society ; of the Divinely ordained group—which Western nations call caste—to which he belongs ; of the village community in which he lives ; of the joint family into which he is born. Apart from these larger wholes, he has no existence.

The practical effect of this Indian outlook is profoundly important, for it has led to a view of human life and of human institutions which is quite different from the accepted ideas of the West. India is a country of communities and not of individual citizens. It is these communities with which the state, in orthodox Indian view, should deal. In consequence the function and the duties of the state in India have always differed very much from its functions and duties in Europe. So large a share of what we should consider typically governmental work is done by the joint family, the village community, and the caste, that before British rule the state hardly came into contact with the individual citizen. In consequence the ideals of co-operation with the authority of the state—of what we term civic consciousness—have never made much progress in India.

For example, although in India it is generally now considered the duty of the state to keep order and to maintain the peace, it is not thought that the individual citizen has a duty to assist it in the task. So if an Indian policeman gets into difficulties, the passers-by seldom think it necessary to help him. " He is doing his work as a policeman, so why should we interfere ? " is perhaps the typical attitude. And this attitude is not confined to British India where the policeman might be considered the symbol of alien rule. It is also found in the Indian states, where for centuries the people have only known the sway of their own rulers. The fact is, there is deep attachment and loyalty to the group—to the joint family, to the village, to the caste or religious community. Here the tie is strong, and, as it were, tangible. But while there is also real patriotism in India, it is patriotism to an idealized " Mother India," and not loyalty to state institutions as such. No doubt this is partly to be explained by the fact that these institutions have generally been in the past, and are indeed largely still to-day, foreign in inspiration. But the full explanation does not lie in this alone : it lies also in that typically Indian view of life, which regards the state as something rather artificial in comparison with the institutions in which the cosmic order is more directly manifested—the joint family, the village, the caste.

Of these institutions the caste is most typical of India. Western scholars have devoted much attention to it, and have given various explanations of its origin. According to some authorities, it arose from the determination of the white-skinned Aryan-speaking people who invaded India some four thousand years ago to avoid being absorbed into the darker-skinned Dravidian-speaking people whom they found then ruling the country. The Aryan-speakers were probably already familiar with such groups as the family, the clan, and the tribe which governed permissible marriages ; and these groups, transported to Indian soil, might have provided the germ from which caste was to grow. According to other authorities, the caste system in its main essentials was borrowed by the white-skinned invaders from their dark-skinned subjects, by whom it had already been developed elaborately from an origin partly totemistic. That the Aryan-speakers were profoundly influenced by the people whom they conquered is, indeed, certain ; for the original Aryan (the word " Aryan " means " belonging to Iran ") deities—" bright " nature-gods rather like those of the early Greeks—were gradually displaced by infinite numbers of gods and godlings, which look as though their origin lay in " darker " and more primitive beliefs. Moreover, the philosophic outlook which we have sketched as typical of much of India is not really an " Aryan outlook " at all, and must have been developed gradually from sources largely non-Aryan.

For even in times as remote as those we are now considering, India was already the home of powerful and tenacious civilizations. Layer upon layer of cultures existed. Of some of these, such as the civilization which flourished in the Indus valley round about 3000 B.C., even the memory had perished, until the spade of the archæologist discovered well-planned cities, elaborate drainage systems, and wealth of artistic development. Peaceful and unwarlike, the men of this Indus valley culture perished, it may be, before the might of more barbarous people. Quite probably the Aryan-speaking peoples themselves, men of the same Indo-Germanic stock as our own ancestors, were mere savage marauders compared with the people whom they subjected. This indeed is a common happening in the long history of India, and no doubt accounts in part for the Indian feeling that the state is an " outside " thing, imposed, as it were, by force, and no part of the institutions which really shape and give expression to social life.

But whether the caste system was devised by the Aryan-speaking invaders, or whether they found much of it already developed by conquered peoples who in their day had once been invaders, its influence has been profound, for it has shaped the socio-religious structure of India for at least three thousand years. To the Western observer its main effect has been to divide society into an elaborate system of some two thousand water-tight compartments, each isolated from the other by fear of ceremonial pollution in connection with such matters as marriage and the taking of food. The whole structure is bound together by religious principles ; by the reverence and respect enjoyed by the priestly class ; by the deep determination to respect one's own caste rules and to avoid infringing the caste rules of other people ; and by the extreme sanctity accorded to certain animals, such as the cow, the monkey, and the peacock.

From our point of view the caste system appears as an iron band of social tyranny, the effect of which is to fix each individual's status, though not perhaps his manner of living or wealth or personal prestige, in accordance with the accident of birth, binding him by formal rules which prescribe and restrict his habits, his marriage, his diet, and even sometimes his occupation. In fact, it seems to us rather terrible ; and we condemn particularly the hopeless degradation imposed upon the so-called Depressed Classes, who are kept outside it by age-old custom.

But, as might be expected, the Indian does not share this view. He often resents our condemnation, and retorts by pointing out that in European society class distinctions are so rigid that in some countries at least they govern marriage and social intercourse as rigorously as does his own caste system. This contention misses the point that under Western conditions an able or fortunate individual is not rigidly bound by limitations of birth, but can enter classes higher in the social or economic grade than those in which he was born ; while under the caste system this is scarcely possible.

The fact to be remembered is that to the Indian, with his cosmic outlook, caste is an institution with a definite biological significance ; indeed a time-honoured system of eugenics. As the ants and bees are specialized according to the function which each inmate of the hill or the hive discharges, so, it is held, should men be bred with the spiritual and physical qualities which their work in life requires. Inherently, at least, the four great divisions have no right to be considered as gradations in the social scale ; they are rather looked upon as necessary parts of a huge organism, of which no part may claim to be more essential than the others. Thus the *Brahmins*, or priests, are equated to the head ; and *Kshatriyyas*, or warriors and administrators, are compared to the arms ; the *Vaisyas*, or merchants and craftsmen, to the legs, and the *Sudras*, labourers and servants, to the feet. In theory, therefore, since all these are required for the due functioning of the social structure, they are all equal in value.

But in India, as elsewhere, modern practice does not coincide exactly with ancient theory ; and the Brahmins and the Kshatriyyas have a marked social precedence over the other two ; the Brahmin in particular being accorded great reverence from the mere fact that he is born a Brahmin, quite apart alike from his personal worth and from whatever calling he may pursue. As an historical fact, castes have come into existence in many different ways ; some castes were originally tribal, as when the Rajput clans, some of whom were doubtless of foreign, and others of aboriginal, stock, became admitted to the fold of Hinduism as Kshatriyyas. Other examples of these are provided by the Marathas of the Deccan and the Jats of the Punjab, separate races which have become separate castes. Other castes were originally occupational, such as goldsmiths, grain merchants, and (lower in the scale) weavers. Still other occupations, such as leather working, are considered degrading ; and those who practise them are outside the caste system altogether.

The caste system does not operate entirely as the Western observer might expect : in some ways it is curiously democratic. Each caste is internally a self-governing and self-ordering community, rather like a guild in mediæval Europe. It imposes on itself, without the assistance or intervention of the state, its own laws through its own committees and councils, on which each member has a vote. The caste is, moreover, a kind of brotherhood, often stretching over wide areas, within which all caste-fellows are equal, regardless of wealth or position in life. The caste also performs charitable functions, and is bound together by common reverence for the caste deity. And curiously enough, the whole system, despite its antiquity, is remarkably flexible and adjustable to new conditions.

For example, the seclusion of women, generally called the *parda* system, which was originally no part of the Hindu social code, was within historic times adopted by certain castes—probably as a defence against disorderly conditions. Again, in our own days, new occupational castes grow up, with their own rules, in response to modern needs. In some parts of India chauffeurs and electricians are now forming something like a caste, and, true to the old principle of specialization, are relegating certain duties, regarded as menial, to other incipient but inferior castes. Also, if a caste abandons an occupation which carries some social stigma, and adopts another, it tends to rise in popular estimation. An increase in the wealth of a particular caste, due to some change in economic conditions, may also raise its prestige ; and it then tends to adopt the social practices of higher castes—for example, the seclusion of women.

Further, without any apparent weakening of the structure, caste restrictions which are found unworkable under modern conditions, for example in railway travelling, are relaxed ; or loopholes are found which make them adaptable. Older people shake their heads, but the new usages are quietly adopted, to become in their turn part of the working system. But the essentials of the system—the determination to marry within the permitted castes, to abstain from ceremonial pollution, and to respect the ghostly power of the Brahmin—are, if anything, reinforced by the modification of non-essentials. Some ancient precepts, however, which have defied modification are now real obstacles to economic progress. Among these may be mentioned the refusal to utilize bone-manure, the refusal to take the life of certain destructive animals, and the preservation of cattle, regardless of the effect upon the breed, which consume more than they produce.

The caste system has often been condemned by Western observers, and, which is perhaps more in point, by many Indian saints and sages in the past. The three great religions which Hinduism has " budded

off," Buddhism, Jainism, and Sikhism, as well as in-
numerable other smaller reforming sects, have all taken
their origin from protests against the caste system. It
is strongly attacked to-day by some social reformers ;
although it is noticeable that the most powerful and
effective criticism is directed rather to the removal of
those features which fail to accord with modern sentiment than to any abolition of the system itself. Despite
all attack, it remains the essential warp and woof of Indian
life. It even exerts an astonishing influence upon those
who are entirely outside the Hindu fold. There are
divisions corresponding to caste among the ranks of the
outcastes. Stranger still, it has even affected the social
organization of both Indian Muslims and Indian
Christians, whose position in India is almost that of
separate nations, sharply marked out from the Hindus
among whom they dwell. An institution at once so
ancient and so vital deserves the respect of every student.

Regarded from the narrower aspect as an instrument
of social integration, the caste is an extension of the two
smaller and more localized groups—the village community and the joint family. The Indian village community is an institution of remarkable interest ; not only
for its antiquity and self-governing institutions, but also
for the fact that almost 90 per cent. of the population are,
even now, villagers. The Indian village is of immemorial age ; and the houses of to-day may often be seen
raised high above the level of the surrounding country
on a mound formed from the débris of unnumbered
earlier dwellings. Much research has been undertaken
into its origins ; but these are so obscured in the mists
of antiquity that little can be stated with certainty.
There are, however, reasons for believing that, in es-

sentials, the village community pre-dates the arrival in India of the Dravidian-speaking peoples, who seem to have used it as an organ of local government.

Originally, perhaps, each village was an independent and entirely self-governing community, with its assembly and " committee of five " (*panchayat*) which settled village affairs and determined difficulties. The officials apparently were paid from lands set aside for the purpose. No doubt taxes had to be given to an overlord, whether person or temple ; but that was almost the only connection the village had with the outside world. But this condition of affairs seems to have come to an end before the invasion of the Aryan-speaking peoples ; for the Dravidian-speakers had already made the village officials into State officials, and assigned to them certain responsibilities for law and order beyond the responsibility owed to the village community itself. The Aryan-speakers seem to have tightened up the system ; and even by the time of the earliest Sanskrit law books the village headman was always appointed by the state. So short are the memories of men that in our own time the British have been accused of ruining the village community because they followed just the same plan ! The truth seems to have been that under any strong system of government, from the third millennium (at latest) before Christ, a well-ordered state has always employed the village as an organ of local government, while still leaving it free to manage its domestic affairs ; but whenever the authority of the state was weak, the village pursued its own way of life, regained its autonomy, and survived in its humble sphere while kingdoms and empires crashed to pieces.

In some parts of India even to-day the village preserves

its ancient characteristics ; it polices itself ; it taxes itself for village purposes ; its council is the tribunal for civil and criminal cases. The old isolation, it is true, is breaking down ; village is being united to village by road, and often by motor bus. New wants are created, and imported articles to satisfy them are everywhere found. The " natural " economy of exchange and barter is being replaced by a monetary economy, with interesting effects upon the social structure of the village. But the village still stands as a community : the village elders still settle village affairs in the traditional way, sitting under the pipal tree at sunset, as the dust of the home-driven cattle slowly sinks and the smoke of the cooking fires rises against the evening sky. So it was before the British came to India ; so doubtless it will be when their direct rule has ceased.

The smallest unit of social grouping is the joint family, which may have been originally an Aryan institution. If so, it has become much modified in India by the communalistic outlook characteristic of the country. Its essence in the common ownership of means of production, and the common enjoyment of the fruits of labour. Both inherited and personally acquired belongings are regarded as common property ; and the supreme authority is the family council, of which the head of the family, generally the eldest male, is the executive officer but not the dictator. The family may consist of dozens of persons, grandparents, uncles, sons, grandsons, with their wives and children ; and the ties of loyalty to which it gives rise are intense. Indeed, to many Indians, the duty owed to other members of the joint family appears something far stronger than any duty owed to the State. What Westerners call nepotism is in India a positive virtue ; a fact which constitutes a frequent source of misunderstanding between Indians and Englishmen.

The joint family, like the village and the caste, shows considerable powers of adaptation to modern conditions, and under the Indo-British legal system has lost some of its rigid communalism. Certain types of property are now recognized as vesting in individuals ; economic changes and the education of women are leading to the slow increase of the " married couple " type of household with which we are familiar in Britain. But the ancient joint family is still immensely powerful, even though its component parts may no longer live under a single roof. Its existence as a social organization seems in little danger, although economically its old ability to support idlers at the expense of their more energetic relatives may be threatened.

But while the outlook of some sixty-eight out of every hundred Indians is based broadly upon the view of life we have described, it must not be forgotten that there exists in India what is virtually a separate nation, eighty millions strong, which adheres to a creed with an essentially Western view of life. The Muslims hold fixedly to the conceptions of a single omnipotent God, of the equality of mankind, and of the dignity of humanity. Their beliefs mark them out distinctly from the Hindus, to whose cherished principles they are fundamentally in opposition.

Islam is relatively a new-comer to India, since it made its appearance during the eighth century, and did not become a considerable factor until the thirteenth. But from that period until the time when effective control passed to the British, the Muslims ruled northern India, where they are still principally to be found, and exercised great influence elsewhere in the country. Every empire which flourished from the thirteenth to the eighteenth century in Hindustan was a Muslim Empire, for during this period all the invading peoples who swarmed through the passes of the North-West Frontier were themselves Muslims ; and there were also powerful Muslim kingdoms in the south. In consequence the Muslims of India have a great tradition of Imperial rule, and are very jealous of such political developments as might subject them to the numerical superiority of the Hindus.

As a community their strength lies in their unity of outlook, which contrasts forcibly with the sectionalism to which Hindu culture seems to lead. They are also deeply conscious of their affiliations with Islam in other countries, and believe that with the assistance of their co-religionists among the frontier tribes, in Afghanistan, and in Central Asia, they could again rule India if the strong hand of Britain were withdrawn. Their weakness lies in the fact that as a community they are for the most part poor and ill-educated ; and while their aristocracy is largely derived from the victorious conquerors of other days, the rank and file are often the descendants of converted Hindus. The original converts were sometimes members of menial castes, or even of aboriginal or depressed classes outside the Hindu fold, to whom conversion represented a rise in status ; and while they firmly hold to their faith, they have tended to infect the community with their own ignorance and fanaticism.

Perhaps as a result of this Islam in India impresses the observer differently from Islam in Turkey, Arabia, or Iran. It is very largely influenced by the Hindu caste

25

system, which it has never been able to obliterate. And though it held political domination over much of India for six centuries, it never succeeded in establishing a true Islamic state, and it never originated any great Islamic movement. In the realm of architecture its achievements were, however, notable. Mighty fortresses, stately mosques, exquisite mausoleums—among which the Taj Mahal, "planned by Titans and finished by jewellers," reigns supreme—rank high among the treasures of India's heritage. Islam remains to-day in most parts of India a minority community, tenacious of its rights and proud of its separate existence—a nation apart from the main cultural tendencies of Hindu India, but commencing to co-operate with it in modern political movements.

The stately structure of the Hindu social system, of which some characteristics have been briefly described, stands forth as one of the most enduring organisms which humanity has ever devised. It has produced—it still produces—saints, sages, philosophers ; from its womb have sprung warriors, statesmen, poets, and even innovators. From it have branched, in the course of centuries, faiths of such significance as Buddhism, Jainism, Sikhism. It has inspired notable works of art ; Hindu architecture, Hindu painting, Hindu music, Hindu literature, both sacred and secular, each deserves and demands a lifetime's study for its due appreciation. It has extended its influence to every part of India. Despite all differences of race and language, the Hindu finds himself at home in every region of the great sub-continent. Wherever he goes, he finds people pursuing the same ritual, revering the same deities, keeping the same festivals, obeying the same caste restrictions, and reciting

—albeit in different tongues—legends of the same heroic figures. The holy places of Hindu pilgrimage are located in some of the extremest geographical limits of India ; yet the pious traveller, whether he is worshipping on the burning sands of Cape Comorin or amidst the frozen snows of Kashmir, finds himself in the company of those pursuing the same devotions. It is these things that convince the Indians that India, despite all social and linguistic divisions, is yet one country.

How is it, then, that with this vast community of age-old culture India has not developed either a national government or a civic sense ?

CHAPTER II

HISTORIC OBSTACLES TO NATIONAL UNITY

WITHOUT some knowledge of Indian history it is hard to understand the difficulties which face the country to-day, or to estimate the prospects that they will be successfully overcome.

We must begin our brief study of India's past with a paradox. Despite the manner in which Nature would seem to have marked out India as a distinct country, despite the manner in which, as we have seen, the characteristic culture of India has permeated to every part, there never has been a government which has ruled the land from a single centre. We British have perhaps come nearer to this ideal than any one else ; but we have not realized it. Even to-day the Government of India rules less than two-thirds of the country. The remaining parts have still their own kings, whom we call the Indian Princes.

It is true that the Princes are in alliance with, and owe loyalty to, the British Crown ; but the territory over which they rule is not British territory, and their subjects are not technically British subjects, as are the inhabitants of British India. In fact, to meet modern conditions, special arrangements have to be made. So far as the outside world is concerned the people in the Indian states rank as " British Protected Persons," although in British India they are eligible for recruitment to the public services.

As is almost always the case in India, there is nothing inherently new in this strange system. As it is with us to-day, so it was with the numerous empires in the past. They have never directly administered the whole country, although they have often exercised a military supremacy over most of it. What has held them back? This is an important question, because if the forces which have frustrated the development of India into a single polity are still operative, the difficulties attending the attainment by India of dominion status as a self-governing member of the British Commonwealth are immensely increased, and may, indeed, prove insoluble.

Broadly speaking, there are three groups of factors which have in the past operated to prevent centralized rule in India ; and they may be characterized as physical, racial, and cultural. These operate in conjunction with one another, and the spheres of their influence overlap. After a brief consideration of them, I think many readers will agree with me that some are still operative, though perhaps in a modified form, to-day ; so that if we were endeavouring even in the year 1938 to set up a governmental machine which would exercise direct rule over all India from a single centre, we should probably find the task as hopeless (though for slightly different reasons) as it was found in the past. Fortunately for every one concerned, the problem, as we shall see, is being tackled in a different way, and one which affords at least the prospect of harmonizing with, instead of running counter to, the factors which have operated so tragically in the past.

We may first examine what, for convenience, I have called the physical factors, although these cannot be isolated, except for purposes of artificial clarity, from the other two. India appears on the map like a rather irregular ace of diamonds. The lower sides are bounded by the sea, and form a coastline more than 3,000 miles long, with very few good harbours—a fact of some importance. The upper sides are defined by mountain ranges which, while not impassable, offer considerable difficulties to free intercourse with the rest of Asia. The area enclosed within these boundaries is about 1,500,000 square miles—roughly equal to all Europe without Russia. From north to south, and from east to west, almost every conceivable variety of scenery, of vegetation, and of animal life can be encountered. In the north extremes of heat and cold are found, and some of the loftiest mountains in the world lie close at hand. The central regions have a typically sub-tropical climate ; here the geological formations, of immense antiquity, are the surviving portions of a great lost continent which once covered what is now the Indian Ocean. In the south there are tropical conditions, with constant heat and considerable humidity.

The effect of these conditions upon the peoples of India is obvious to any one who makes a railway journey from north to south. The contrast, both in physique and in mode of life, between the warlike, primitive, and turbulent inhabitants of the north-west, and the gentle, highly civilized, and peaceable inhabitants of the south, is more marked than any difference between the peoples of Europe. Almost equally striking is the contrast between the truculent, hardy desert-dwellers of Sind in the west, and the peaceful, laborious toilers in the rice-fields of Bengal. But although these differences in physical type may be accentuated by the climatic variation, they are not entirely due to its influence.

The peoples of India are divided into well-marked national units, with their own traditions, literatures, and languages. Some of these national groups, like the Rajputs, the Sikhs, and the Marathas, have proud traditions of imperial rule, which are written in crimson letters across the scroll of Indian history. Others, like the Bengalis, have excelled most in the arts of peace, and have built for themselves a heritage of artistic achievement, of which they are justly proud. Still others, like the Dravidian-speaking peoples of the far south, or the Gujarati-speaking peoples of western India, have traditions of overseas and domestic commerce which extend unbroken from epochs long before the Christian era. There are many other communities, which together constitute a kind of living museum of culture, stretching almost from the Stone Age to the twentieth century.

The most primitive stock recognized by ethnologists has been termed Indo-Negroid; dark-skinned people like the negroid types of Africa and Melanesia. Not much more advanced in the scale were the peoples now represented by such jungle tribes as the Irula of the Nilgiri hills, who, it is believed, came originally from the north; and the mixture of these two types with numerous subvarieties has produced a type of " aboriginal " clearly distinguishable from the other Indian peoples. The second main stock, termed comprehensively the Melanids, comprises an important group of Dravidian-speaking peoples, the Tamils in the far south and the Mundra tribes in the north-east highlands of the Deccan. It has been conjectured that Dravidian speech was imposed upon them by invasion from the north ; but this is uncertain. The third main stock is that of the Aryan-speaking peoples, who never succeeded in spreading themselves over the whole country, but only in part permeated through the Deccan to southern India. They are represented by two separate types ; one small-boned and " gracile," the other taller and bigger-made. In addition, there is a fourth, Mongolian strain, introduced from the north-east, which has greatly influenced the physical type now found in the Himalayan foothills, in Assam, and in Bengal.

The linguistic differences are as well marked as the physical and cultural differences. In all, there are about twelve main languages,[1] while distinct dialects number more than two hundred. Religious divisions are less numerous, but unfortunately give rise to great bitterness. Roughly speaking, out of every hundred persons, sixty-eight are Hindus, twenty-two are Muslims, three are Buddhists, three follow some more or less primitive tribal religion, one is a Christian, and one is a Sikh. Of the two others, one may be either a Buddhist or a Christian ; while the last may probably be a Jain or a Parsi.

How did this bewildering mixture of peoples, races,

[1] The language with the widest currency is Hindustani, in its two forms and scripts Hindi (Hindu) and Urdu (Muslim) : but this is far from being understood all over India. In the south there are four important Dravidian languages—Telugu, Tamil, Kanarese, and Malayalam. Fifty million people speak Bengali. Marathi is the language of parts of the Bombay Presidency, the Central Provinces, Berar, and Hyderabad. The Punjab and Kashmir speak Punjabi. Gujarati is widely spoken in Western India ; Rajasthani in Rajputana and Central India. Leaving aside special dialects and remote areas, a man who desires to make himself generally understood in most parts of India needs to know as many languages as there are in Europe.

and languages come about in a country which looks as if it were intended by nature to be self-contained, if not entirely uniform ? The reply to this query lies in the fact that the history of India is primarily a history of invasions; but that these invasions have never been sufficiently complete in their effects to hammer conquerors and conquered into racial unity. And the underlying explanation is largely physical. Invaders have been obliged by nature to follow three main routes ; for the practicable passes across India's mountain barrier are limited in number. In the extreme north the mountains are impracticable for invasion *en masse*, although adventurous travellers can find their way from India to China and back by this route. On the north-east the ingress, though difficult, is practicable ; the Mongolian peoples have penetrated through the passes into India, where they now constitute a distinct element in the population. But in the north-west the way lies open to the invaders, and through the passes which lie between Afghanistan and what is now called the North-West Frontier Province, invaders have passed one after another since the dawn of history. Farther south lies the Bolan Pass, which was once of great importance before climatic changes made Sind a desert ; but in historic times it has not been much used by invaders because it does not lead to any wealthy or attractive part of the country.

Now the fact that invasions always took place through rather difficult mountain routes has profoundly affected the nature of the invasions themselves. For while these routes are quite practicable for armies, they are very difficult for great national migrations. The hardships are great, and many of the women and children among the invaders must have died. There was thus, almost of necessity, a mingling of strains, at least among the non-aristocratic classes, between the invaders and the invaded. But the mere fact that this mingling was necessary was possibly among the reasons for the invention or adoption of the caste system. Threatened with absorption, the invaders took drastic steps to limit and control the process. In so doing they effectively prevented complete fusion. And when the caste system was once in operation it would function almost automatically to preserve the identity of the later invaders, either by excluding them from the fold altogether if they were Muslims, or by relegating them into a separate caste if their culture was of a type less strongly marked. The tendency, in fact, was for each successive invader to constitute, as it were, a dominant caste. All this would tend towards the subjugation rather than the disappearance of the peoples whose territory was invaded. Added to which, the country itself is very large, and its vital centres lie far away from the gates which give access to invaders. The natural desire of the invaders to drive out or to exterminate those who resisted them could not long have been effective. The victors would soon become content with submission, servitude, or tribute. In this way even the conquered peoples would retain much of their old manner of life : and being in superior numbers, would tend to preserve their speech and culture.

At this point a further consequence of the difficulties of the path to India must be noticed. The mountains which made the invasion difficult and dangerous, even when successfully accomplished, would cut off the invaders from the land whence they had originally proceeded. In other words, India has acted as a kind of labyrinth ; not very easy to get into, but almost impossible to get out of. The invaders had nothing to do but to make the best of new conditions. They had come to seize India ; India in turn seized them—and kept them. Their own country knew them no more.

Now if the conditions of life in India had resembled the conditions in which the invaders had originally lived, this " cutting of the painter " would not have mattered so much. But every one of the peoples who have invaded India, at least in historic times, has come from lands where the climate was much more rigorous, and where conditions of life were harder. It may be that to this climate and to these conditions they owed the mental and physical vigour which made the invasion successful. However this may be, peoples whose home is in the temperate zone, whether of Europe or of Asia, have always found the Indian climate enervating, and the Indian ways of life insidiously attractive. They have thus tended, in course of time, to lose their primitive vigour. Cut off from their own land by the mountain barriers, they had little chance, unless they were sufficiently strong to hold both sides of the passes, of recruiting their own kith and kin to fill the gaps in their fighting line. To hold both sides of the passes entailed the maintenance of long and intensely vulnerable lines of communication, and no invader succeeded in doing this for any length of time.

Yet such recruitment was the only means by which their dominance could be secured, for success and luxury weakened their fibre, just as the Indian sun—so curiously and markedly inimical to inhabitants of the temperate zone—thinned their blood. Lacking this reinforcement the invaders became assimilated to and mastered by the conditions of their new home. The native powers, once subdued, began to raise their heads ; internal troubles threatened. The domination of the invaders has now settled down into one of the empires of which India has known so many. And before long history repeats itself ; another set of invaders, themselves fresh and vigorous, come storming through the gates of the North. The resistance of the invaded is again overcome, and the same process begins all over again. It has not happened only once or twice ; it is a tragically recurrent feature in the record of India.

Thus, leaving aside those racial elements which must have entered the country before the dawn of history, we know certainly of invasions by Aryan-speakers, by Persians, by Greeks, by Scythians, by Huns, by Turks, by Afghans, by Tartars, by Mongols.

Perhaps a particular example will make this curious cycle more vivid. In the middle of the reign of Henry VIII., a central Asian Prince of Turkish extraction, called Babur, descendant on the male and female side of two great conquerors, Timur and Chengizkhan, invaded India and founded the great and glorious Mughal Empire— more formidable, more civilized, more populous, more cultured than anything that contemporary Europe could boast. He also brought with him the fashion of portrait-painting, and for the next two centuries we have excellent portraits of many of the important aristocrats. The nobles who came with him, as well as his soldiery, were fine, tall, upstanding men, with ruddy cheeks and strong beards, armed with great swords, and striding about in leather jerkins and high riding-boots. They were men of outstanding hardihood ; and Babur himself swam every river he crossed on his road to Delhi. Within the next generation or two the sons and grandsons of these

" ruddy men in boots " have become very different-looking people. They have abandoned their jerkins and their boots ; they are now clad in beautiful muslins, and on their feet are jewelled slippers. Gone is the great sword ; in its place is only a dainty, slender blade. If we pass on another generation or two, what do we find ? " Pale persons in petticoats," elegantly smelling a rose !

No doubt the degeneration did not proceed so quickly among the rank and file ; for the Mughal emperors held the gates of the North for the better part of two centuries, and while they did so, were able to recruit some of the stoutest fighting men in Asia. But just about the time when bad internal disorder in the shape of the Maratha uprising under the famous national hero Shivaji threatened Aurangzeb, the last great Mughal emperor, frontier troubles prevented him from recruiting the one class of warriors who might have given him the victory, the mountaineers of Afghanistan. In consequence, the Mughal Empire began to weaken; internal discord grew more serious ; new invasions completed the fatal cycle. Nor did the Marathas profit by their success to bring India under their sway, although at one time they looked like doing so. For circumstances brought them face to face, first, with an invasion from the North of the old type, which seriously weakened them, and then with an invasion of a wholly different type, which at length subdued them.

This new type of invasion, of which we British were the exponents, introduces a fresh factor into the operating causes which had hitherto shaped India's history. This factor is sea power. Until the middle of the eighteenth century all the many empires which India had known were based primarily upon military, as opposed to naval, power. But with the entry of the European nations upon the Indian scene we begin to trace the effects of the new factor. Even when the British in India were a handful of traders, operating only by the contemptuous toleration of the Great Mughal, Aurangzeb, a dramatic illustration of sea power occurred.

In 1688, driven to desperation by the exactions of the Mughal officials, the East India Company engaged in hostilities against the emperor. The relative resources of the parties were ludicrously unequal. We should have something like a parallel to-day if the principality of Monaco were to declare war on France, or if Luxembourg were to proceed to hostilities with Germany. The emperor promptly expelled the English from Bengal and besieged Bombay. To all appearance they were ruined. But although they were helpless on land, they caused the emperor the most active inconvenience by sea. They cut off all trade with the West ; worse still (for he was a pious Muslim), they rendered the pilgrim traffic to the Hedjaz impossible. Hence, when they realized that they had underestimated his strength, and sought to end the war, they found him most ready to show himself accommodating ; and at the cost of a fine received all their trading privileges once more, and had far less trouble with the imperial officials for the rest of Aurangzeb's reign.

In an increasing degree, as the eighteenth century proceeds, are the destinies of India linked with the control of the surrounding ocean. Because the Portuguese, the Dutch, and the French successively lost their sea dominion, the British stood out supreme above their vanquished rivals. Further, as the British period of Indian history began to develop, it became clear that command of the sea gave the new-comers a power of mobility and a security of operation that no rival whose resources were based primarily upon land dominion could hope to emulate. Sea power appears to turn the flank, as it were, of the difficulties which had always in the long run proved fatal to invaders by land. Nature remains the same. The Indian climate is no more friendly to the British than to the Mughals ; indeed, the British have probably inferior power of resisting its influence. But sea power has enabled the British to do what neither the Mughals nor any earlier invader could ever do, namely, to rule India without making it their home.

Modern Indian critics of British rule in India take it as a grievance that we have never attempted to make our home in the country ; that we have never established ourselves, as did all previous invaders, as a people at one with, if superior to, the peoples over whom we rule ; that we have clung fast to our own land and have not been content to see ourselves just one more racial element in the ethnological hotch-potch of India. The critics have failed to perceive that in this has lain not only the very essence of our power, but also one potent cause of the emergence of the modern Indian sentiment of nationalism, which, in opposition to a Western culture perpetually rejuvenated from its source, and thus unblurred by Indian conditions, has begun to transcend the age-long separatism of the races and languages for which India is a home.

This healthy stimulation, reinforced, as we shall see in a later chapter, by Western educational and political influences, has been a continuous and cumulative process, the effect of which has been permitted full play by the peace and order which Britain has brought. For while the control of the sea rests with the British, their communications with their own temperate land cannot be severed by any mountain barriers. Exhausted men can be sent back to recuperate ; fresh men can supplement the gaps in the fighting line. New resources can be brought to bear continuously until opposition is worn down. Indian powers could, and often did, defeat us on land, but, as one of the greatest of our opponents, Haidar Ali of Mysore, remarked on his deathbed, it was idle to resist us unless the sea could be dried up, for we would never be the first to weary in any struggle.

We have now seen how the natural influences of the Indian frontier and of the Indian climate have operated, in conjunction with the advent of successive waves of invaders, to fill India, before the coming of the British, with a multitude of separate nationalities, which have been preserved from effective fusion by the working of the caste system. A certain amount of fusion did, of course, take place in practice ; but it was not sufficient to destroy the identities of the parties to it. Moreover, the country itself is so large that a nationality which found itself in danger of extinction could generally preserve itself by abandoning the territory it held, and retiring to some less attractive locality where the invader of the moment could not, or did not desire to, follow it. It is no exaggeration to say that to-day, even after the lapse of hundreds of years, it is possible to find in India racial types representing the descendants of almost every invading people of whom history tells us.

The tendency towards political separatism resulting from the diversity of races, and the difficulty of any one racial element completely dominating the rest, have been powerfully reinforced by the influence of those curious social institutions which we examined in the first chapter. We saw that the characteristic culture of India is communalistic rather than individualistic ; and that the joint family, the village, and the caste have from time immemorial done much of the work which in the West has always been done by the state. The result has been to confine the state's function in India, in pre-British times, to such matters as external defence (or aggression) ; internal co-ordination ; and revenue collection. Thus successive invaders were able to settle down, as it were, to the enjoyment of a ready-made administration, which provided them with a sufficient revenue without any other obligation than that of being strong enough to insist that it was paid. The state, so to speak, sat on the top of the whole structure ; the real work of administration—or a large proportion of it—was done almost automatically from below.

As we saw in Chapter I., the "artificiality" of the state as compared with the "reality" of the subordinate organizations—family, village, caste—is a characteristic of the Indian outlook on life. And the influence of this, politically, has been very great. These three "real" institutions tend to function best among kinsmen, and to operate most efficiently through small areas. Thus the most vital political institutions of the country stopped short at what we in the West would call local government, and accordingly local government units tended to multiply and to take political shape as little kingdoms. These little kingdoms, which were the highest form of political integration compatible with traditional ideas, were greatly encouraged by the size of the country and the continual addition of new racial elements resulting from invasional history. They therefore held their position with great tenacity, and each successive empire had to take account of them. If they resisted an invader in the first flush of his strength they could, of course, be conquered ; but they could rarely be destroyed. In practice it was generally found most convenient to demand submission, tribute, and military service.

As a consequence, no empire in India from the Mauryas, whose Persian-inspired dominion flourished from 322 B.C. to 185 B.C., to the Marathas, whose hey-day overlapped the commencement of the British period, ever found it possible to govern directly more than a small portion of the total area which owned its sway. The great Buddhist emperor, Asoka, 273 B.C. to 232 B.C., one of the most attractive and wonderful figures in the history of the East, overlord of a larger portion of India than is directly administered in the name of our King to-day, was still dependent upon local kingdoms for the detailed work of governing, and without their co-operation could not succeed in his aims. Even the greatest and most highly organized empire of all, that of the Mughals, with its impressive list of viceroys and governors, was obliged to content itself with the tribute and submission of the subordinate kingdoms. The emperor Akbar (1556–1605), wise, humane, and tolerant, saw so clearly the importance of the local kingdoms that he determinedly set himself, by marriage alliances, by the bestowal of generous confidence, and by the conferment of high official rank and responsibilities, to bind the Rajput kings to his throne. In this he largely succeeded.

Asoka and Akbar, in their very different days and ages, found the path of wisdom. Others were less prudent. If at any time an attempt was made to centralize administration by force of arms, the result was generally

fatal to the empire which embarked upon such an undertaking ; for it dissipated in the task the resources which
it required both to maintain its supremacy internally,
and to defend itself against the fresh invaders hammering
at the gates of the North. The results of such a policy
are suggestively shown by the tragic failure of the
emperor Aurangzeb's attempt to conquer the little
Muslim kingdoms of the Deccan. By destroying the
existing equilibrium he not only released the forces of
the Maratha national revolt, but he so weakened the
imperial structure that shortly after his death such
imperial viceroys as the Wazir of Oudh and the Nizam
of Hyderabad threw off the yoke of Delhi and became
independent sovereigns ; while three disastrous invasions
in twenty years completed the ruin of the imperial
fabric.

It is important to realize that imperial sway in India
has always involved a curious kind of unstable equilibrium. Many empire-builders have preceded the
British, some native, some foreign ; Mauryas, Sakas,
Kushans, Guptas, White Huns, Rajputs, Ghorides, Slave
Kings, Khiljis, Tughlaks, Afghans, Mughals, Marathas,
Sikhs. All have encountered, and eventually succumbed
to, the same difficulties. The forces making for dis-
ruption were very powerful ; the little kingdoms with
their separate national identities and separate national
cultures ; the politico-social institutions which produced
strong local patriotisms. Yet empires have proved
necessary for the well-being of the country ; for during
those periods when there has been no power strong
enough to keep the peace, to enforce submission, and to
collect tribute, internecine wars have usually occurred
between the little kingdoms, and the condition of the

country as a whole has been most miserable. But, on the other hand, when any empire has attempted to suppress local patriotism, to obliterate local culture, and to destroy local units of political integration, the result has been equally unhappy. A deep-seated malaise has spread through the whole fabric. Desperate revolts have occurred, and again anarchy has ensued.

Our brief summary of the reasons why India has never been directly administered from a single centre, and has never given birth to a unified national state such as alone could evoke an active civic consciousness, is now complete. In a sentence, the explanation lies in the fact that local patriotisms, based through historic circumstances upon differences in race, culture, and language have been too strong. Had the country remained undisturbed these differences might not, in the course of ages, have prevented such reasonable accommodation between the races as would, at long last, have favoured the production of a living national entity. But the integrations of indigenous elements were perpetually disturbed from without by armed invasion, and by the introduction of cultural elements, such as Islam, which have proved in whole or in part unassimilable.

It seems too much to expect that a national racial type will now evolve. The diverse ethnic and cultural elements have enjoyed their separate existence too long. Their perpetuation must be recognized, for the immediate future at least, as inevitable ; and a place must be found for them in any political integration which is to endure. But when once this attitude of mind is adopted the situation appears full of hope. To abandon the conception of uniformity is probably the first step towards achieving a national synthesis which at once recognizes and utilizes diversity. Local patriotism can be made the basis of a higher political integration, which is now for the first time rendered possible by the existence of modern means of communication and of a *lingua franca*, in the shape of the English language, common to the leaders of each administrative area or racial group. Finally, the irritant of a dynamic Western culture, impinging upon a cultural tradition to different, has encouraged sectional groups, in face of their Western rulers, to stress their common similarities rather than their age-old distinctiveness.

There is thus no reason to suppose that India cannot attain political unity, provided that this unity is in a form compatible with national diversities. But for this accommodation to be achieved there is one essential condition. There must be a governmental system sufficiently strong to maintain internal peace, and sufficiently formidable to render external invasion too hazardous to be attempted.

CHAPTER III

TWO PRE-REQUISITES OF POLITICAL INTEGRATION

THERE is an obvious conclusion to which a study of Indian history inevitably leads : namely, that the two most formidable obstacles to the political integration of the country have been recurrent armed invasion and recurrent internal disorder. On more than one occasion, when the indigenous elements seemed upon the point of creating an all-India policy which, allowing the necessary play to the local political forces, would permit of a superior synthesis expressive of fundamental unity, the incursion of a new ethnic element has reduced everything to confusion once more.

We have already noted that these invasions have often seemed to coincide with the weakening of a once-dominant empire through internal stress ; but closer examination shows that the pressure on the frontier has been almost continuous ; and could only be resisted by strenuous and ultimately exhausting efforts, which drained the vitality necessary for the maintenance of internal order. It is indeed a remarkable fact that before the British imposed their peace over the land, India has scarcely ever known an unsuccessful invasion. The great emperor Chandragupta Maurya (322–298 B.C.) did, it is true, repel an incursion of Seleukos Nikator, and drive him beyond the frontier. The mighty Muhammad Ibn

Sam, who founded the domination of Islam in northern India, did suffer one temporary check at the hands of a Rajput coalition in A.D. 1191. But these are mere isolated exceptions to the general rule that those who have invaded India have succeeded in what they set out to do, whether their aim was the conquest of a province, the acquisition of plunder, or the founding of an empire. In view of this fact, it is the function of defence which must first claim our attention.

The problem of defending India has always loomed large in the minds of those who from time to time have exercised domination over the country; and the British have not escaped the anxieties which were so familiar to their predecessors. We have already noted that they have so far enjoyed one advantage which preceding empires have missed—command of the sea. But this advantage has been accompanied by a corresponding responsibility.

Since the rise of modern sea power, India's long coast-line, rare harbours, and rich sea-borne trade have combined to make adequate marine protection a necessity. The connection with the British Commonwealth has hitherto assured this; but the exploits of the German cruiser *Emden* during the war of 1914–18 showed how vulnerable India may prove to be if the command of her seas passes even momentarily into the hands of her enemies. So long as the naval power of the British Commonwealth remains adequate to the discharge of its responsibilities, it seems unlikely that India will have to reckon with invasion from the sea. This point of view was for so long firmly held that until recently it was regarded as axiomatic; and India's contribution to her own naval defence was formerly limited to a token payment of £100,000 a year towards the expense of the East Indies Squadron of the British Navy, and to the maintenance of a transport and survey service dating back as far as the seventeenth century, known as the Royal Indian Marine.

But of late Indian aspirations towards an increasing responsibility for the defence of the country have been gratified by the remodelling of the Royal Indian Marine upon a combatant basis, and by its recognition as one of the unitary fighting forces of the Empire. The British Government has now arranged with the Indian Government that the token payment shall cease, in return for India's undertaking to maintain a minimum number of six armed vessels. The Indian Navy is designed rather for co-operation with the British Navy than for independent offensive action ; and the most that it could do would be to assist in defending such major ports as Bombay, Calcutta, Karachi, Madras, and Rangoon. But its mere existence is interesting for two reasons : first, as providing a means of reviving the ancient sea-going tradition once typical of certain Indian peoples, who in days gone by carried the glories of Hindu culture to Indo-China and the islands of the Dutch East Indies ; and secondly, as showing that the importance of India's sea defences has not escaped the notice of those who realize that aspirations towards self-government must connote increasing responsibilities for self-defence in every field which modern international conditions can affect. Recruitment for the Indian Navy is good, and a very fine type of young seaman, both of the officer and of the lower-deck class, is being trained.

But the aspect of India's defence problem which still looms largest is that of safeguarding her frontiers from invasion by land. The defence of the North-East Frontier has now ceased to be a primary responsibility of India herself, for with the emergence of Burma as a separate political entity, the protection of that frontier will fall in the first instance to the lot of the Burma defence force. The defence of the North-West Frontier, however, still presents itself with all the traditional grim intensity.

The land between the Indus and the passes, despite the fact that it is celebrated in Sanskrit literature as the earliest Indian home of the Aryan-speaking peoples, and indeed, as the cradle of Hindu culture, now seems scarcely to belong to India at all. It seems designed by nature to form the muster-ground of invading armies when once they have forced the mountain barriers ; and it is full of the descendants of former conquerors. Through history it has fluctuated in its political adhesion, sometimes looking beyond the mountains to Kabul and the Central Asian hinterland ; sometimes attaching itself to India. It was a province of the Persian Empire under Darius. It became part of India under Chandragupta Maurya. Shortly afterwards it was incorporated, along with Kabul, in the Buddhist Empire of the Kushan kings. But since the conversion of Central Asia to Islam, this tract has always inclined to turn its eyes beyond the passes. The Mughal Empire held it for a time ; but in the eighteenth century it again became part of the Persian Empire of Nadir Shah, whose savage sack of Delhi in 1739 has caused his name to serve in Northern India, even to-day, as a synonym for brutal cruelty. After his death Ahmad Shah, who in 1761 broke the Maratha power in the terrible fight at Panipat, bound these tracts to his new Afghan kingdom. Then came the rise of

Sikh power under the great Ranjit Singh (died 1839), who drove the Afghan armies beyond the passes and won their exits once more for India. To the Sikhs succeeded the British; so that the trans-Indus country has now been united to India for a little less than a century.

It is not an easy unity; and were it not for the necessity of holding the passes, the temptation to retire beyond the Indus would be great. With the exception of a few Hindus located in the more peaceful areas, the inhabitants of what is now called the North-West Frontier Province are mainly of Turco-Iranian stock, far more closely allied to the inhabitants of Afghanistan than to any of the peoples of India. They dislike all systems of government except their own fierce tribal custom; they are impatient of authority, and regard murder as a pastime. They have been accustomed for centuries to prey upon their weaker neighbours. To control them is a heavy task, costly in lives and in money. But it must be faced. A river is never a good frontier; further, if India's control over the trans-Indus districts were relaxed, an admirable base for large-scale invasion as well as for small forays would be vacated, to the great encouragement of those who gaze upon the peaceful plains of India with avid eyes. There is, in fact, no option in this matter; the trans-Indus country must be held, for to hold it is the only way of securing incomparably the most dangerous frontier in the British Empire, beyond which, banked up as water is banked up by a dam, lie age-old savagery and brutal, ruthless fanaticism.

The British learned these facts by hard experience. To begin with, we attempted a policy of non-interference with the tribes, contenting ourselves with holding the plains into which the passes debouched. The Amir of Kabul claimed, but did not exercise, authority over many of the clans bordering upon our territory, whose raids called for perpetual punitive expeditions. Behind Afghanistan lay Russia, always ready to use a threat to the North-West Frontier as a move in the game of European politics. Hence much trouble, some of it no doubt unnecessary, between British India and Afghanistan during the nineteenth century. As a result of the Afghan War of 1878-79, we secured control of the Khyber Pass, the Kurram Valley, and further south, the Bolan Pass ; but we still made no attempt to dominate the tribal country.

The claims of Afghanistan to a vague overlordship remained a perpetual source of trouble until the demarcation of the British-Afghan spheres of influence by the fixing of the " Durand Line " in 1893. The Amir of Afghanistan, by a series of ruthless operations, carried his authority effectively up to the newly demarcated boundary. We refrained, deterred largely by consideration of valuable lives, expense, and parliamentary criticism, from doing the same thing on our side of the line ; save in one area—Baluchistan, where simpler conditions, exploited by the genius of Sir Robert Sandeman, carried our authority right up to the Afghan border. Thus the north-western portion of the frontier is still divided into two distinct spheres : the so-called " settled districts," which are under direct British administration, though governed largely in accordance with tribal custom ; and the " Independent Territory " between the " settled districts " and the Durand Line.

The terrain of the " Independent Territory " presents appalling difficulties even to modern operations. The lines of access are strictly limited and readily defensible. Enormous hills, narrow gloomy valleys, impenetrable caverns and crevasses, together constitute an ideal field for guerrilla warfare and a corresponding handicap to large-scale expeditions. Even the air arm is severely handicapped by dangerous air currents and by the ease with which powerful contingents of tribesmen can conceal themselves in the broken ground.

There has been much controversy as to the best method of dealing with the " Independent Territory," which is not really independent at all, since it is subject, in a degree which varies from time to time, to British control. The old " close border " plan, by which we left the tribes alone until their depredations became intolerable, and then, with one eye on the Indian taxpayer and the other on the House of Commons, launched an expensive little punitive expedition, proved a costly failure, for it did nothing to bring the tribes to a more settled way of life. The newer plan has been to occupy strategic points in tribal territory, to open up the country by roads, which tribal levies are well paid to patrol, and to find means of relieving the bitter poverty which inflames the tribesman's traditional propensity to enrich himself at the expense of more peaceful and prosperous neighbours.

Already large numbers of tribesmen come to India in the cold weather to seek employment of various kinds. They act as watchmen ; they peddle trifles ; they lend money ; they work in mills. But they will not, if they can help it, endure the heat of the plains during the summer ; and the first onset of the hot weather finds many of them again in their hills. Each village is a stronghold ; each house is a fort. Fields have to be cultivated with rifles ready to hand. There is no law but that of keenest eye and the quickest trigger-finger.

It may be that this state of affairs will not continue indefinitely. In the "settled districts" education is beginning to exert its influence and has resulted in a demand for political reform. The Pathan is essentially democratic and is not content to be left behind when other Indian provinces are becoming autonomous in local affairs. As a result of his political agitation the "settled districts" of the North-West Frontier Province have now a constitution which corresponds *mutatis mutandis* with that of the other units of British India. For the moment the party of advance works with the Indian National Congress to increase "popular" control. But its real strength lies in its link with the border tribes. Will these at length become civilized—yet another element in the catholic structure of a united India—or will their traditional point of view prove strong enough to wean the "settled districts" from the path of constitutional aspirations to the world-dream of pan-Islamism?

It must be remembered that there is little distinction in race, habits, or disposition between the inhabitants of the "settled districts," the tribes in "Independent Territory," and the tribes in the Afghan sphere beyond the Durand Line. All are ready, if they think they discern any weakening of control, or if they are moved beyond caution by some outburst of religious fanaticism, to make common cause, at least for the moment, against the forces of law and order. The Afghan administration naturally perceives in this situation a valuable element in its own security, and is by no means reluctant to countenance the support of the tribes on our own side of the border line. Thus the frontier is never really at rest, and " local trouble " is always to be expected.

The potentially formidable character of even purely local trouble can be estimated from the fact that the inhabitants of the territory between the Indus and the Durand Line number between five and six million, with a fighting strength of about a million and a half, a large proportion of whom are armed with modern rifles of great range and precision—without such a weapon no Pathan is considered a man. But it is not merely the local trouble which has to be considered by those upon whose shoulders the responsibility for defending India rests. There is the further fact that this uneasy land is the link between India and Central Asia, still a hive of predatory peoples, large tracts of which are at present under the influence of a great Power whose future evolution and present policy are by no means calculable factors.

" It is noteworthy," observes the Report of the Indian Statutory Commission, " that notwithstanding the teeming millions of India's population, comparatively small bodies of invaders have often succeeded in overcoming all opposition and making their way through to the plains, where they have established themselves as conquerors. It is the difficult and necessary rôle of the Army in India to guard against a repetition of these dangers." [1]

This army consists of some 60,000 British troops and 150,000 Indian troops, commanded mostly by British officers—one fighting man to every 1,280 civilians, without including some R.A.F. formations stationed in the country. Its size is certainly not unreasonable in view of its responsibilities ; but it is very costly in proportion

[1] Cmd. 3,568 (vol. i., para. 114).

to the public revenue of India ; for military expenditure amounts to some £34 million a year—nearly 30 per cent. of the combined budgets of the central and of the provincial governments. Even this figure can only be adhered to as a result of unremitting economy.

The necessity of employing so many expensive British troops—each British soldier costs between three and four times as much as each Indian—is often questioned by the Indian Nationalist, who sees in their presence merely a means of perpetuating British domination. He asserts that India cannot afford them ; and is made to pay for them, not because it needs them, but because Britain prefers to maintain them at his country's expense. He maintains that Indian troops are quite capable of defending India. On these points he is entitled to his own opinion, although the record of history is against him on the last.

But there are two facts of which his criticism does not take account. The first is that " Indian troops " belong to a very few classes and communities, and do not represent the masses of the population. The second is that the utility of the British soldier to modern India consists not only in his professional military capabilities, but in the impartiality which enables him, standing as he does outside the borders of Indian castes and creeds, to exercise these capabilities in a way which convinces the public that his action is free from bias. Both facts merit a short explanation, for they are intimately connected with the second part of the problem now being examined—the maintenance of internal order and tranquillity.

It might be deduced from Indian history (although many Indian leaders to-day bitterly resent the deduction) that a very large proportion of the peoples of India have no military tastes and little military capacity. India has not followed the lead of China in ranking the soldier as the meanest of mankind ; on the contrary, the warrior-class even now come next to the Brahmins in prestige, and at one period, apparently, took precedence over them. But the fighting castes have always been specialized, and comparatively limited in numbers ; and the other castes have always been taught that military prowess was no concern of those for whom custom had not prescribed it.

Nevertheless certain parts of the country and certain communities breed fine soldiers. Military traditions are very strong in many Indian states, where there is a warlike aristocracy and a keen clan-spirit. Certain of the rulers maintain well-equipped forces which they place at the disposal of the King in time of need ; and the great majority of the states have a fine record of military co-operation with the British. During the last war, for example, many states rendered great services ; and the names of the rulers of Hyderabad, Bikaner, and Patiala—to mention three only—became household words in Britain. So far as British India is concerned, fighting men are naturally more numerous in the north of India, where successive invaders have settled, and where the mastery of the country has so often been decided. The result is seen to-day in the fact that 77 per cent. of the Indian Army come from the North-West Frontier Province, the Punjab, and the United Provinces (62 per cent. come from the Punjab alone), while all the rest of India supplies only 23 per cent. Bengal, with a population of 50 millions, scarcely provides any combatants.

There is thus a clear distinction between the martial and non-martial races ; the former despise the latter, and would dominate them if they could. The military classes do not shine intellectually, and are not examination minded. The Indian intellectual, on his side, has as a rule no taste for a military career. Muslims constitute about one-third of the Indian troops ; two-third are Hindus and Sikhs. All alike tend to be impatient of " government by discussion," for the sword is their heritage. It is true that the British have been accused of deepening the division between the martial and the non-martial races by confining their recruiting to the former. No doubt there has been a tendency to recruit from the races which offer the best fighting material—the practical risks of any other policy would have been great. But it is very doubtful whether the old clearly marked distinction could have been blurred by any action of the British. Further, it was noticeable that during the most critical stages of the last war, when it can hardly be suggested that recruiting was discouraged in any area, the Punjab and the United Provinces produced three-quarters of the total number of recruits.

The history of India shows that the division of the total population into fighting and non-fighting peoples holds two serious dangers. One is that the fighting peoples should engage in internecine warfare for the mastery of India, a thing which the small local kingdoms —often now represented by the Indian states—were always prone to do ; the other is that they should oppress their unwarlike neighbours. It cannot be stated with any confidence that either danger has disappeared in the course of the three generations of effective British rule. The former is still a possibility if British authority were withdrawn. In conditions which they regarded as holding a prospect of success, the Muslim community

would probably, with the assistance of their co-religionists beyond the passes, make a bid to regain the mastery
they held for so long ; while the Hindus and Sikhs,
conscious of their numerical superiority, would actively
resist such an attempt, and themselves endeavour to make
India a Hindu land. In the welter of warfare that would
follow, the second danger would materialize, and the lot
of peaceful persons would be miserable.

All these are unpleasant possibilities ; and to take them
into account is to run the risk of being called reactionary.
But the present writer can vouch for the fact that during
the period when British fortunes seemed at a low ebb
during the war of 1914–18, such contingencies were
actually discussed by Indians of power and position; and
a working alliance, implemented by a strategic plan, was
arranged to secure the dominance of one party over its
rivals by force of arms. It is to be hoped that such a
situation will not again occur. But the practical importance of the possibilities we are considering is that they
emphasize the necessity, for the present at any rate, of
the British soldier.

The second fact which justifies the maintenance of
British troops is the tension between different religious
communities. The most common and the most dangerous form assumed by this tension is strife between Hindus
and Muslims, although " domestic " rioting between
rival Hindu sects is not unknown ; while the differences
between Muslim sects also tend to bloody affrays. In
normal circumstances, particularly in the villages and
small towns, Hindus and Muslims are neighbourly
enough ; and although their habits and ways of life
present extreme contrasts, so that the Muslims generally
prefer to live all together in a separate street or locality,

they exercise a good deal of mutual tolerance. Moreover, the leaders of both communities often join hands in political agitation against the British, and at such periods an observer who does not know India might be inclined to consider that the importance of communal differences has been exaggerated.

But from time to time a wave of fanaticism sweeps over one or the other community, particularly in large towns where men do not know their neighbours so well. The occasions for such fanaticism are manifold. The cow is sacred to the Hindus, but the Muslims practise cow-slaughter ceremonially. The Hindus like music in all their processions ; this interrupts Muslim prayers in the mosques, where music may not be used. The Muslims carry lofty structures of tinsel and wood in the Mohurram ceremony ; these structures are too tall to pass under the sacred banyan and pipal trees so common in Indian towns ; the Muslims will not lower the *tazias*, the Hindus will not allow the branches to be cut. Moreover, Hindus and Muslims follow different calendars, so that important festivals sometimes coincide. Again, there are frequent causes of friction in the economic sphere. The Indian peasant (as we shall see in Chapter VIII.) is often in debt to the moneylender. The moneylender is usually a Hindu ; his debtors may be Muslims. Sometimes the situation is reversed ; but the result is the same—the hatred felt for the money-lender is transferred to the community to which he belongs. There is also keen competition between the two communities for posts in the administration.

From these and many other causes feelings become inflamed, and in the twinkling of an eye a riot starts. Advantage is promptly taken of the confusion by roughs and gangsters, and forthwith the forces of law and order are fighting desperately to restore the peace. Often in such circumstances the military authorities have to come to the aid of the civil police ; a step to which the public are well accustomed, and which, indeed, the peaceful citizen promptly demands. It is at such junctures as these that the British soldier is invaluable. He is quite impartial, being neither a Hindu nor a Muslim ; he is very good tempered, does not lose his head, and has enormous self-control under provocation. For which reason, doubtless, there are approximately 35,000 British as against 30,000 Indian troops earmarked for internal security alone.

It will thus be seen that the problem of maintaining internal peace and order through a country so vast as India, inhabited by so many different races, and containing so many elements of potential conflagration, is just as serious as the problem of securing the frontiers from armed invasion. The British have often been accused of fomenting communal differences, on the " divide and rule " principle, to maintain their own power ; but the charge will not be endorsed by any one who has practical experience of the difficulties to which the administration is exposed by these recurrent disturbances. Every British officer, civil as well as military, dreads them. Whatever happens, he stands to shoulder the responsibility and to bear the blame. He is certain to be the target of interested attack from one side or the other, while his own superiors will be among his most exacting critics. To accuse the British of fomenting communal disturbances deliberately is to speak either in ignorance or in malice.

Nevertheless it is a fact that they have increased of

late. And the reason is plain. The advent of democratic forms of government has placed a premium upon political agitation, and neither Hindus nor Muslims are willing to lose an opportunity of demonstrating the importance of their communities. A spirit of competition has been engendered ; leaders on both sides appeal to the masses of their co-religionists for support ; organized groups exist like the Hindu Mahasabha and the Muslim Khilafat Committee, which conduct propaganda against one another and strive to claim the allegiance of the " depressed classes " by " reclamation " to Hinduism and by " conversion " to Islam. The prizes of the contest are place, power, and influence. So the communities draw apart, feelings rise high, and some small incident precipitates a crisis. It is these new conditions—these growing-pains of a new political order—which are responsible for the increase in communal bitterness.

Where these conditions do not exist affairs go on better. For example, in the Indian states, communal disturbances are rare, though unfortunately less rare than formerly. Broadly speaking, the explanation lies in the fact that under the rule of Indian Princes neither community has anything to expect by making itself troublesome or anything to fear from the predominance of the other. Disorder is firmly repressed by the administration ; each party knows its place in the state, and knows further that this place cannot be improved by agitation, whether on democratic or on other lines. Occasionally the violent currents of communal politics in British India impinge upon the comparatively placid waters of a state ; and then the result may be disastrous, as was recently the case in Kashmir and, though under different circumstances, in Alwar. But the tact and firmness which characterize so many Indian rulers generally prevent agitation within state borders—where it has no prizes to gain at the expense of the rival community—from coming to a dangerous head.

Steadily ranged as they are on the side of law and order, if sometimes rather a traditional law and a static order, the Indian states constitute a valuable stabilizing influence in the internal politics of India. It is possibly significant that they are among the strongest believers in the value of the British soldier to India at the present juncture. Indeed, the peaceful security of a self-governing India would be exposed to great risks, if it relied for the purpose of defending its frontiers and maintaining internal order upon Indian troops drawn from selected areas and special races.

The problems which we have been discussing in this chapter are as delicate as they are important. The undoubted difficulties attending the dual task of safeguarding the frontier and of maintaining internal peace are admitted by many Indian leaders, but the British are often accused of magnifying them. It is a fact that in the past those who regarded Indian political aspirations as dangerous have found in these difficulties their most formidable argument in support of unmodified British rule, with the natural result that Indians, in a wholly understandable impatience, sometimes tend to minimize the ever-present risk to external security and internal order. Indians also accuse us of keeping in our own hands the work of defence, and then using their military unpreparedness as a justification for denying them self-government. Accordingly there is a keen agitation for the " Indianization " of the army—by which term is meant the replacement of the British officers in Indian regiments by Indian officers ; and for the provision of an Indian-officered artillery and air force.

It is plain that a self-governing India must eventually be responsible for the defence of its own frontiers, and for the maintenance of internal tranquillity. Nevertheless it is a long, and probably protracted, road from the present position to the formation of an Indian national army, drawn from India as a whole, in which every member will recognize the rest as his comrades, in which Indian officers will lead men who may be of different races and creeds, and in which public opinion will have general confidence. That the establishment of such an army should be the goal of both British and Indian military policy can hardly be doubted, but it is unfortunate that while a beginning has already been made, it was not made earlier. In fairness to British soldiers and statesmen, however, we must remember that the aim of " responsible government for India " was only laid down as recently as 1917, and that the world-situation during the intervening period has increased those risks which any large-scale experiments in " Indianization " are held by expert opinion to entail.

Before the last war the only Indian officers were those who held what was called the Viceroy's Commission. They were mostly promoted from the ranks, and though widely respected as fine soldiers, were comparatively uneducated ; typical members of the fighting races which despise book-learning. No doubt had the Indian intelligentsia displayed any taste for a military career, the system would not have lasted so long. As it was, it was only in 1918 that Indians became eligible for the same kind of commission as is held by British officers. Vacancies were thereafter reserved for members of the educated classes at Sandhurst and at Cranwell, and since then an Indian Sandhurst has been established at Dehra Dun. Five infantry battalions, two cavalry regiments, and a pioneer unit were selected for transformation into units officered exclusively by Indians; and by about the year 1946 the process should be complete. This scheme has since been expanded to embrace an entire division of all arms and a cavalry brigade. In 1935 the Indian Regiment of Artillery was formed, the first unit of the regiment being a field artillery brigade. Territorial battalions have been established up and down India, and cadet corps attached to the universities.

These innovations, though they may strike the British as real and even daring, are regarded almost with contempt by the Indian Nationalist. Naturally impatient to grasp the substance of power, the whole problem of defence and security is a very sore point with him. He greatly resents the fact that even in the Federal Constitution laid down by the 1935 Act, the control of the armed forces vests in the Governor-General and not in the Federal Cabinet ; and he is exasperated by the slow and cautious manner in which Indianization is being achieved.

On the other hand, one advance of supreme importance has been made in the Act of 1935 : the function of law and order in the provinces has been made over to cabinets responsible to the elected legislatures. This means that while the troops will for the present at least remain under ultimate British control—although there can be no doubt that the Governor-General will act in the closest possible collaboration with the Federal Ministers—the policing of the country will be the responsibility of the popular governments in the provincial units. Quite possibly these governments will before long wish to raise local defence forces, on a territorial basis, to assist their police in times of stress. Such a step will not only relieve the local governments of the necessity of invoking the aid of the regular army under Federal control, but may also provide a new basis for the creation of a national Indian force, at least for internal security. For reasons already noticed there will be formidable difficulties, but an obvious line of advance seems here indicated.

The army in India has splendid traditions, of which it may be justly proud. It has often rendered assistance to Britain beyond the confines of India proper ; although, of course, when it does so, the cost falls upon the British, and not upon the Indian, Exchequer. Its services during the last war were invaluable. At a very early stage of hostilities 21 cavalry regiments, 69 infantry battalions, and 204 guns were provided. Before peace was declared, more than one and a quarter million men, combatants and non-combatants, of whom nearly a million went overseas, had come to the assistance of the Allies. It is devoutly to be hoped that no such emergency will again arise, for the army in India has a great part to play in building up the political future of the country.

It seems indeed clear that the function of the British soldier in India to-day, and of the Indian Army as now constituted, is to hold India's frontiers and to maintain internal security, while behind the shield thus constituted the foundations of a national army are being laid. We may conclude this brief survey of the problem by quoting the wise words of the Indian Statutory Commission :

" We are only concerned here to convey a double warning—a warning on the one hand that Britain cannot indefinitely treat the present military organization of India as sacrosanct and unalterable, but must make an active endeavour to search for such adjustments as might be possible ; and a warning on the other hand, that Indian statesmen can help to modify the existing arrangement in the direction of self-government only if they too will co-operate by facing hard facts and by remembering that those who set them out for further consideration are not gloating over obstacles, but are offering the help of friends to India's aspirations." [1]

[1] Vol. i., para. 126.

CHAPTER IV

THE SCAFFOLDING OF MODERN INDIA

IN previous chapters we have investigated some of the reasons why India has never known a national government. From the standpoint of the student of political institutions, her whole long history may be regarded as a record of frustrated endeavour, which contrasts tragically with her notable contributions to the world's heritage of art, learning, and philosophy. We have seen that she has never enjoyed a sufficiently protracted period of peace, untroubled externally and internally, to enable her to grapple successfully with her quite uniquely difficult problems of domestic co-ordination.

The supreme contribution made by the British to the Indian peoples has been security abroad and peace at home. Scarcely less important has been the stimulus imparted to the spirit of nationalism, liberated for the first time by these favourable conditions.

Before tracing the rise and growth of this spirit, we must briefly survey the nature of the dominion under whose protection it has made its appearance. Such a task necessitates a short account of the methods by which British rule in India came into being.

The East India Company sprang directly from the triumphs of England on the sea in the Elizabethan era ;

and it was on the advice of Drake himself that the great Queen granted the first charter. The British were somewhat late in the Eastern field ; the Portuguese and the Dutch were well established. None of these three nations had any idea, at first at least, of founding an Eastern Empire. It was trade that attracted them ; for such commodities as spices—a necessity of life when every one lived on salted meat and dried fish during the winter—could be had very cheaply indeed in the East, and could be sold for a great price in Europe. The Dutch, who were the strongest of the three at sea during the first half of the seventeenth century, paid little attention to India, and moved further East to the " Spice Islands," whence they expelled their rivals and laid the foundation of the great dominion—more than half as large as the U.S.A.—now known as the Dutch East Indies.

The British were stronger than the Portuguese, and so secured supremacy in Indian waters. They obtained leave from the Mughal Empire and from the local kingdoms to trade and to establish small factories ; and for more than half a century were successful in adhering to the policy tersely laid down for them by Sir Thomas Roe, sent as their ambassador to the Court of Akbar's son, Jahangir (emperor, 1605-27), namely, to maintain no garrisons and to embark upon no land wars. The first British " factory," or trading station, was founded at Surat in 1612 ; Madras was established in 1640 ; a settlement was permitted at Hooghly in Bengal in 1650 by a grateful Viceroy who was cured by one of the Company's surgeons ; Bombay, which had come to Charles II. as part of the dowry of his Portuguese queen, was rented to the Company in 1668. All these places, it should be noticed, were of no military and little commercial importance. They were chosen because they could be reached and supplied from the sea.

But before very long the internal disorders into which the Mughal Empire was falling compelled the British traders to consider plans of defending themselves and their goods. They accordingly began to make their warehouses defensible. When the home authorities remonstrated, they were told that the only persons who could live undefended in India were such as were " stick-free and shot-free and such as could digest poyson." As the arm of the Mughal Empire became weaker, its local officials and local feudatories threw off their allegiance, and disturbances became frequent. Before the end of the seventeenth century the Company, much against its will, found itself obliged to convert its " factories into forts " and to recruit garrisons, which were soon put into uniform as a method of advertising British cloth. At length, exasperated by exactions, the Company was rash enough, as we have already noticed, to declare war on the Empire itself. Thanks to the effect of its sea power, it was able to escape ruin, and even to improve its position in Bengal, where the fortitude and enterprise of the famous Job Charnock, " always a faithful man to the Company," resulted in the foundation of Calcutta.

The Mughal Empire before long entered upon its death throes. The ensuing anarchy reacted in different ways upon the three localities where British settlements were established. Madras was remote from the main currents of Indian politics, and until galvanized to action by rivalry with the French, lived a fairly peaceful existence in the shadow of two strong powers ; the independent kingdom (now known as Hyderabad) established by the former Mughal viceroy of the Deccan, Asaf Jah ; and his great feudatory, the nawab of the Carnatic. The early Nizams of Hyderabad were engaged in almost constant hostilities with the Marathas, and had little time to spare for the humble trading stations of the foreigners, who accordingly encountered no worse trouble than that of defending their walls from marauding gangs. Bombay was less fortunate. It was exposed to attack, not only by the formidable Maratha power but also by the naval dynasty of the Angrias, once Maratha admirals, who declared their independence and set up as piratical princelings. The British found it necessary to maintain a strong fleet and a garrison of over 2,000 men ; thanks to which they gradually won the respect of the Marathas and were allowed to trade so far as trade was possible.

It was from Bengal that the British really rose to power in India under dramatic circumstances. This province was among the last to yield to the universal disorder ; indeed the local Muslim governors were so strong that they oppressed both Hindu and British traders with impartiality. For some time the Hindus hoped that deliverance would come from their Maratha co-religionists, but this hope was not realized. The British grumbled and protested, but were powerless to do more. At length the succession to the governorship of a weak and vicious man, Siraj-ud-Daula, brought matters to a head. He quarrelled with the leading Hindu financiers ; in 1756 he attacked and captured the feeble defences of the English citadel, Fort William, in Calcutta. Many of the British fled down the river ; a certain number of prisoners perished in the first of a number of tragic occurrences which still hold embittered memories for British or Indians.

Siraj-ud-Daula was not himself responsible for the

" Black Hole " incident, in which 146 prisoners were incarcerated in a guard-room through a stifling night, so that only 23 came out alive ; his subordinates were stupid and callous rather than deliberately cruel. One of the survivors, Holwell, was gifted with a powerful pen and a lively imagination—so lively that attempts have subsequently been made to discredit his testimony. But the main facts are borne out both by the narratives of other survivors and by official Dutch records kept in the adjacent factory of Chinsura. Great indignation was excited both in England and among the Company's servants elsewhere in India ; a fact which goes some way to explain, during the next few years, a change for the worse in the attitude of the British towards the Indians. As it happened, owing to events quite unconnected with affairs in Bengal, the British were in a position to exact prompt and terrible vengeance.

It will be recalled that during the middle decades of the eighteenth century France and Britain were engaged in a deadly duel for colonies and possessions almost all over the world. As it happened, India became the scene of some incidents in this struggle. France possessed small settlements in Bengal and on the Madras coast ; and two French administrators of great ability, Dumas and—above all—Dupleix, determined to extirpate British power in the latter region. Looking back upon the struggle which took place between 1744 and 1756, we can see that the French had no chance of ultimate success ; for, except on rare occasions, they were not in a position effectively to dispute the command of the sea with the British. But they endeavoured to redress this weakness by acquiring political influence on the land. They trained considerable bodies of native troops in European discipline, and were thus able to intervene in the domestic quarrels of the local Indian potentates.

With these tactics the British were for some time quite unable to compete ; for the French Company was really a subordinate branch of the French Government, and was staffed by soldiers and diplomats, while the servants of the English Company were traders. The British were thus gravely embarrassed, until circumstances disclosed the exceptional military genius of an obscure clerk named Robert Clive. He mastered French designs both in war and in diplomacy ; established the British as one of the principal powers in the south ; caused their alliance to be sought by powerful kingdoms ; convinced not only his own troops but also hostile forces that the star of good fortune invariably presided over British arms ; and after a series of spectacular triumphs with inadequate resources, became while still a young man a national hero. At the moment when the Calcutta tragedy occurred, he had just returned with a great reputation to India. He brought with him considerable forces, transported on a powerful fleet commanded by Admiral Watson. He was armed with instructions to complete the ruin of French power in India.

He commanded the land forces in the punitive expedition now despatched from Madras against Siraj-ud-Daula ; Admiral Watson was in command of the fleet. British naval skill was decisive. The dangerous channels of the Hooghly River were traversed, the troops were landed, and Admiral Watson's battleships turned the flank of Siraj-ud-Daula's forces. The governor of Bengal was quickly brought to terms : full compensation, the restoration of all privileges, the permission to refortify Calcutta. The combined naval and military forces then drove the French from Bengal. Siraj-ud-Daula longed to intervene against the British, but was paralysed by the news of Ahmad Shah Durrani's sack of Delhi in January 1757, which led him to fear that he might be the next objective of Afghan invasion.

The governor was feared and disliked both by the Hindus and the British; and as a result of a series of dubious intrigues was defeated by the British under Clive at Plassey, and replaced by a relation, Mir Jaffar, who was entirely in the hands of the Hindu-British coalition. Clive's own part in the proceedings, apart from conspicuous military gallantry, was marked by reprehensible trickery. Wealth was showered upon him by the new governor; the Company was given revenue rights over a large tract of territory; and the dues payable to the governor as a condition of the grant were made over by Mir Jaffar to Clive himself. The Company, thanks to these military achievements, was now the dominating power in the great province of Bengal. The British were no longer humble traders, existing on sufferance, they had become possessed of powerful armed forces. From this time onward many of the best mercenary soldiers in India flocked to take service under "leaders who always paid and usually won, and whose own countrymen did the hardest fighting" (Sir Alfred Lyall). Thus the Company became one among the numerous powerful states then existing in India.

Hitherto, it must in fairness be recognized, the Company had conducted its enterprises in India according to principles which combined prudence with humanity. It made no professions of altruism, but it had a lively sense of its responsibilities towards the native population. Its instructions from England to its servants in India, written, not for publication to the world but for the practical guidance of its employees, are sufficient to dispel the common charge that the Company was concerned only to wring every rupee possible out of India. In 1714 the directors wrote : " We have always recommended to you to see justice administered impartially to all and speedily, to govern mildly and yet preserve authority. We have reason to add it here again for your remembrance and earnestly to desire you will take care that none under you be suffered to insult the natives." A little later, having received complaints about extortion, the directors ordered a strict inquiry, and added : " Remember whoever is specially authorized thereunto and doth not act uprightly and heartily in relieving the oppressed brings upon himself the guilt of that oppression : which will prove a load too heavy to bear perhaps in this life when his conscience is awake, but to be sure in that day when the secrets of all hearts shall be laid open and all the actions of men's lives accounted for at an unerring and just tribunal."

These admonitions were, it is true, the outcome of deliberate policy. The directors aimed to make the British settlements secure as well as prosperous. This could only be done if the native as well as the British inhabitants were well treated. In 1721, writing to Bengal, the directors noted, " Security of protection and freedom in liberty and property with due administration of justice must of necessity people your territories considering the country about you is under a despotic government." The Company did its best to see that the administration of its own possessions proceeded along constitutional lines. Municipal corporations were set up in the three " presidencies " of Madras, Bombay, and Bengal ; and in 1726 a Mayor's Court was given to each by Royal Charter. Moreover, the British "presidents," or governors, of the settlements were associated with councillors, and all important questions were settled by a majority of votes.

The progress of this sober and commendable system of administration was for a time interrupted by the events in Bengal, which suddenly elevated the Company into a territorial power, and compelled it to take measures to secure itself from the hostility or jealousy of other powers in India. Unfortunately, public life in India was at that moment much degraded. The Mughal Empire was the shadow of a name. The Marathas and the Afghans were tearing at each other for the mastery of Hindustan. Military adventurers pillaged the country at the head of armed bands. Everywhere there was chaos. There was no public spirit, no order, little honesty. The Company's servants, particularly in Bengal, were not strong enough to resist the general corruption. A short period of great misgovernment ensued ; for while the British enjoyed the substance of power, erecting and deposing their puppet rulers, they had in theory no responsibility for the government of the extensive territories subject to their influence. One of these deposed governors received support from the nawab Wazir of Oudh—a powerful prince whose house, like that of Hyderabad, had seized a former viceroyalty of the Mughal Empire—and even from the reigning emperor himself. But this formidable combination was defeated in 1764 in the bitterly contested battle of Buxar, and the Company remained stronger than ever.

Clive, himself the instrument of the unbelievable change which had come over the Company's fortunes, was the first to point a way to reform. As early as 1759 he had judged that the power acquired by the Company was too great to be wielded by any mercantile concern, and had suggested in a letter to Pitt that Bengal should be taken over by the British people. For the time the suggestion was not adopted—unfortunately for all concerned. Clive afterwards endeavoured to regularize the position by obtaining from the Mughal Empire a grant of the revenue administration of Bengal ; and he laboured hard to put down corruption among the Company's servants by obtaining for them salaries which would place them beyond the reach of temptation. But such a notion was too revolutionary to find acceptance ; the directors would not face the expense involved. As a result, corruption and maladministration continued until the Company got into grave financial difficulties while its servants were making enormous private fortunes. It was obliged to apply to Lord North's government for a loan.

Feeling was growing in England against the Company ; partly on account of the inflated wealth of the " nabobs " —its retired employees—and partly on account of scandalous rumours that the good name of Britain was being imperilled. Parliamentary Committees investigated the situation ; it was realized that the Company's position was due in large measure to the support it had received in time of crisis from the armed forces of the Crown. Public opinion was thoroughly roused. Parliament asserted its supremacy over the Company by resolving that all acquisitions made by military force or by treaty with Indian Princes belonged to the state ; and that the appropriation of such acquisitions by persons entrusted with civil or military power was illegal. Clive's own conduct was severely criticized ; he was acquitted by

Parliament, but the ordeal broke him. Parliament then proceeded to subordinate the financial, civil, and military affairs of the Company to the control of the ministry of the day ; to appoint a Governor-General for Bengal with four councillors to control him ; to establish a Supreme Court for Calcutta.

All this was in 1773—just sixteen years after the battle of Plassey. So short was the period during which there was " exploitation " of a vicious character.

But much remained to be done before real order could be introduced into Bengal. Warren Hastings, the Governor-General appointed under the Regulating Act of 1773, laboured hard to bring peace to the land. He took the bold step of assuming the whole of the civil government of the province as the only way of escaping from the fatal duplication of authority between the Company and the Indian governor ; although for some time the administration of criminal justice remained in the hands of native officials. He suppressed anarchy and set his face against corruption. In the words of a recent writer [1] : " He found the English in Bengal a source of disaster and misery to the country, apparently incapable of cure ; he turned them into a spring of new life which brought integrity and vigour into its government, humanity into its law courts, freedom into its markets. He found the natives themselves, quite apart from the intrusion of the English, hopelessly divided. Had there been no Plassey, Bengal must still have been a prey to anarchy ; rival princes disputed the throne ; marauders drained the most fertile provinces ; official corruption and greed exploited instead of protecting the peasantry. All this was transformed by Hastings ; a firm authority

[1] Monckton-Jones, *Warren Hastings in Bengal*, pp. 319–20.

was set up ; enemies were shut out, and, above all, the long-suffering ryot (peasant), whose cause Hastings had most at heart, learned that he could work his land un-hindered and enjoy a fair share of its fruits, and that poor as well as rich could get hearing and receive justice." When reviewing his work preparatory to retirement in 1786, Hastings wrote : " I have at least had the happiness to see one portion of the British dominion in India rise from the lowest state of degradation."

Unfortunately the British found it impossible to con-fine themselves to the task—of itself overwhelming—of administering efficiently their Indian possessions. They had now become a state in India ; by no means the greatest, and by no means the most influential, but en-joying a firmer foundation of power than any of the others. They had entered, as it were, upon the sphere of high politics, and in that sphere they had to struggle desperately for existence. Bombay became involved in difficulties with the Marathas, Madras with Mysore. Hastings had to face dangers from every quarter ; dis-sensions with his colleagues ; a conflict of jurisdiction with the Supreme Court. By boldness and enterprise he triumphed everywhere, but in so doing he adopted some expedients which his admirers must ever regret. The incidents of the Rohilla War, of the Begams of Oudh, and of the death of Nandkumar, though due in large measure to the desperate situations which from time to time confronted him, shadow the reputation of the greatest Governor-General Britain ever sent to India.

The Act of 1773 did not work well, and in 1784 a new measure was framed to render parliamentary super-vision more effective. Real power was now concen-trated in a Board of Control, whose orders—in reality the orders of the President, who was a member of the Cabinet—were transmitted to India through a secret committee of the board of directors of the Company. In India, Madras and Bombay were definitely subordinated to Bengal; and the Governor-General, who, it was assumed, would have the instructions of the Cabinet to guide him, was given authority in case of emergency to override his colleagues. The Company still retained all its patronage, and even a theoretical power to recall the Governor-General. But in effect the affairs of the British possessions in India were taken over by the Home Government; while parliamentary supervision was ensured by the investigations attending the periodical renewals of the Company's charter. A great object-lesson of the extent of the change was provided by the impeachment of Warren Hastings. This ended—and deservedly—in an acquittal; but it revealed the defects of the system which Hastings was called upon to administer, and it brought home to public opinion some notion of the great responsibilities which British initiative and British determination, operating in a land six thousand miles away, had now laid upon the shoulders of the British people.

These responsibilities involved two tasks of immediate importance, in the fulfilment of which the British dominion in India rose to supremacy. The first was the good government of the territories subject to British authority; the second was the defence of those territories from the other Powers exercising rule in India. These two tasks could not always be separated, although both Parliament and Company struggled hard to do so. It was officially laid down that " to pursue schemes of conquest and extension of dominion in India are measures repugnant to the wish, the honour and the policy of this nation." Lord Cornwallis, the first of the long line of Governors-General henceforth to be selected, according to a wise practice, from English public life, confined himself so successfully to much-needed reforms of the administration that he was almost indifferent to the relations of the British with the other "country Powers" in India. From his time can be traced the foundations of the system of government in India as we know it. He insisted upon substantial salaries for the Company's servants, and enforced, in return, the most absolute integrity. He reorganized the judiciary, set up civil courts in every district, established a proper gradation of courts of appeal, and took into British hands the administration of criminal justice. He also reformed the land revenue system, although his plan, devised to encourage stability and assure proper development, of converting the contractors, who collected the revenue and paid from the proceeds the Government's dues, into landlords with hereditary rights, has been much criticized.

His concentration upon domestic reforms, rather to the neglect of high politics, laid up difficulties for his successors ; for the British gained the reputation of being hesitant and unreliable allies. Another great struggle in Europe between France and England gave an opportunity to the former country to rally certain Indian states which were jealous of British strength. The Marquis of Wellesley (Governor-General, 1798–1805) threw himself with energy into the task of combating French influence. He was entirely successful. He overthrew the usurping Muslim dynasty in Mysore ; he bound the Nizam firmly to the British by an arrangement (technically known as a

" subsidiary alliance ") under which Hyderabad subordinated its foreign relations to British control, in return for a guarantee of security and the service of troops ; he temporarily broke the power of the Marathas. Scindia of Gwalior, Holkar of Indore, and Bhonsla of Nagpur, together with the Peshwa of Poona, were compelled to enter the sphere of British influence after some desperately contested engagements. Wellesley's aim, in his own words, was " the prosperous establishment of a system of policy which promises to improve the general condition of the people of India and to unite the principal Native States in the bond of peace under the direction of the British power." But there was a reaction against this vigorous policy, which was costly and seemed likely to involve the Company into assuming responsibilities which it did not desire. Accordingly, for the best part of the next decade, " non-intervention " became the watchword.

The British, however, had now become the strongest power in India ; and according to the traditional ideas of the land, it was their business to impose order, whether they desired to do so or not. The solid wisdom underlying these ideas was shown by the state of affairs existing about the year 1810. A wedge-shaped block of British territory then extended from its base in Bengal to its apex near Delhi ; there was a further block in the south, connected to Bengal by a narrow coastal strip. There was a smaller block near Bombay. Outside these domains anarchy raged. The Maratha powers were oppressing Rajputana and Central India ; the Gurkhas of Nepal were raiding even British districts ; the Burmese were threatening the North-East Frontier. Fortunately the North-West Frontier was secure, for it was guarded by the warriors of the Sikh confederacy under the leadership of the great Ranjit Singh, " the Lion of the Punjab," with whom the Company had concluded an honourable alliance in 1809. But the condition of the major part of the country was lamentable, and people complained bitterly that the British, though as the strongest Power they were the natural guardians of peaceful persons, refused to use their influence for the protection of weak states from cruelty and oppression.

Before long the Company, as well as British public opinion, realized that it was impossible to call a halt to the progress of British power until peace and order were imposed upon the country. When the Company's charter came up for renewal in 1813 a significant thing happened—it lost its monopoly of Indian trade, and became a definitely administrative and political machine ; a device, in fact, for governing the British possessions in India without the direct interposition of the Home Government. The first Governor-General under the new system, Lord Moira, better known by his later title of the Marquis of Hastings, found that the policy of non-intervention, in addition to exposing much of India to bitter anarchy, was menacing the security of the British possessions by encouraging the activities of a host of enemies. The Maratha confederacy was threatening hostilities. The Gurkhas were actually invading British territory.

Stern and prompt action now replaced hesitancy. The Gurkhas were defeated and converted into firm friends. The Maratha confederacy was broken. Subordinate alliances were concluded in great numbers with states up and down India. " British peace " was laid upon a solid foundation. " Henceforward," to quote the words of Sir Alfred Lyall, " it became the universal principle of public policy that every state in India (outside the Punjab and Sind) should make over the control of its foreign policy to the British Government and should defer to British advice regarding the internal management so far as might be necessary to cure disorders or scandalous misrule." The task of pacification was henceforth pursued unrelentingly, and according to modern ideas, often with too little consideration for the rights of local dynasties. Sind was annexed in very unscrupulous fashion in 1843. The Sikh confederacy fell to pieces after the death of Ranjit Singh, and two tremendous campaigns, probably the hardest fighting the British have ever done in India, resulted in 1849 in the annexation of the Punjab—an event which the British, so far from seeking, endeavoured to avoid. Oudh, now completely surrounded by British territory, was annexed, rather discreditably, in 1856. A number of small states, which were regarded as owing their survival to the action of the British, were incorporated in the Company's territory when direct succession failed. This was an outrageous violation of the Hindu religious sentiment which prescribes adoption as a sacred duty if there are no heirs male of the body. In all these cases the British considered, not without reason, that the course they followed redounded to the advantage of the population concerned.

Thus the map of India assumed the colours we see to-day, and the portion coloured red became the larger part of the country. But, as we have already noticed, more than one-third still remains outside the boundaries of British rule.

CHAPTER V

THE EVOLUTION AND THE NATURE OF THE
BRITISH POLICY IN INDIA

In the last chapter we have traced the process by which the British, partly out of design and partly owing to the influence of circumstances, imposed their rule upon a large portion of India, and asserted a domination which, after initial difficulties had been overcome, gave the country internal peace and a reasonably secure frontier. We have now to examine certain characteristics of their rule, for it was these characteristics, impinging upon the traditional culture of the country, which stimulated, partly by the irritation they aroused, and partly by the emulation they induced, the nationalist movement which we see in India of to-day.

It has been said that the British acquired an empire in India in a fit of absence of mind. If by this is meant that we did not set out with the desire to become masters of India, it is true. But from very early times the East India Company considered its Indian settlements as permanent possessions, to be well governed, to be stoutly defended, to be retained as a part of England. Even in 1687 the directors laid it down as their policy to establish " a well-grounded, sure English dominion in India for all time to come " ; and to this end all their admonitions were framed. But four generations later, when the

British had become the greatest power in India, and the Company itself an instrument of British rule, a significant limitation was imposed upon the endurance of the British dominion in India by some of the shrewdest intellects of the day. The clear-sighted Elphinstone wrote in 1819 : " If we can manage our native army and keep out the Russians, I see nothing to threaten the safety of our Empire—until the natives become enlightened under our tuition, and a separation becomes desirable to both parties."

Munro, whose name is honoured equally with that of Elphinstone among the great administrators who laboured in the newly-acquired territories of the Company, wrote in 1824 : " We should look upon India not as a temporary possession, but as one that is to be maintained permanently until the natives shall, in some future age, have abandoned most of their superstitions and prejudices and become sufficiently enlightened to frame a regular government for themselves and to conduct and preserve it. Whenever such a time shall arrive, it will probably be best for both countries that the British control over India should gradually be withdrawn. That the desirable change may, in some future age, be effected in India there is no cause to despair. Such a change was at one time in Britain at least as hopeless as it is here. We shall in time so far improve the character of our Indian subjects as to enable them to govern and protect themselves."

These two pronouncements are worthy of careful study, for they supply a key to much that has since happened. In the first place, the attitude of detached superiority characterizing the authors was for long typical of Britain's dealings with India. It has not assisted in securing the co-operation of proud and sensitive peoples in action which is inspired, even transparently, by the desire to promote their welfare. It is the more significant as displayed by men who must be ranked with the truest benefactors India has known. They were among the most distinguished of a notable corps of administrators which brought order and peace to millions who for two or three generations had known nothing save anarchy and oppression. But perhaps the very nature of their work, magnificent as it was, inclined them to forget that India, though at the moment suffering from the heritage of disorder, had passed triumphantly through many such periods in its history ; and that similar tasks of reconstruction had been performed on previous occasions no less successfully, if perhaps rather differently, by native administrators—for example, the Mauryas, the Guptas, Sher Shah Sur, Akbar—who were possibly guided by knowledge more exact. While we may well be proud of the work of reconstruction which the British have accomplished in India, we must beware of falling into the error of supposing that we are the only people who have ever ruled India well. Our truest title to fame rests upon the fact that we are the only people who, because of certain novelties both in our manner of rule and in the culture upon which it is based, have put India into the way of ruling itself.

The second noteworthy point about these pronouncements is the unhesitating manner in which they assume that the natural outcome of British rule must be Indian self-government. This assumption is broadly characteristic of all subsequent speculation as to the future relationship between the two countries, although it seems often dependent upon the implied condition that India cannot be self-governing until it becomes more like England. But Elphinstone and Munro differed from later thinkers in that they considered political freedom for India postulated a severance of the connection with Britain. They could not envisage the future emergence of the Commonwealth conception; a larger unity within which separate nationalities can achieve the perfection of their growth. To them, empires were merely the seed-pods of nations, doomed to split asunder as the seeds waxed and prospered. Before their eyes was the precedent of the United States of America, whose people, of pre-dominantly British stock, had severed political connection with Britain and erected out of British colonies the foundations of an independent power. It was some such destiny, unquestionably, that Elphinstone and Munro foreshadowed for India. Dare we yet say with confidence that they were wholly wrong ? It still lies with us to convince the peoples of India that the Commonwealth conception is adequate to their needs.

The distress and anarchy into which India had fallen immediately prior to the emergence of the British as the principal power in the land, enabled us to impress our ideas more deeply upon the country than many of our predecessors had succeeded in doing. From the military point of view, there was no one to oppose us. We ruled directly a larger territory without intermediary than any preceding empire. We had a more unquestioned su-premacy over the subordinate kingdoms with whose presence we were equally unable to dispense. And we were conscious of a wide lacuna in the political structure as we observed it. The caste system was still in being ; the joint family existed ; the village community, al-though in many places temporarily obliterated by anarchic conditions, was still a vital stock. But there was nothing to correspond with what we British, accustomed as we were to the centralized institutions of a small island community, could recognize as the State. The higher integration of governmental activities was in eclipse, except in so far as it was represented by the internal structure of the Indian states. And even they were essentially institutions of local provenance. They did not deal with the larger problems of the country. In British India there was no state at all. We were obliged to create it, so far as conditions allowed, upon the only lines familiar to us.

Of necessity, therefore, we were convinced centralizers, and planned to break down the barriers which had always in the Indian scheme of things separated the activities of the state from the life of the individual. The consequences of this policy were important ; and will be traced on a later page. For the moment, it will suffice to notice that, quite understandably, we fell into the habit of believing that we could mould the great and ancient land of India, with its deep-seated culture and manifold peoples, to our own ideas. We have not succeeded in this, though we have laboured hard to achieve it. But in the course of our endeavours we have contributed notably to India's own heritage.

The spirit of confident benevolence in which the British undertook their immense task may be illustrated by a letter written in 1818 by Lord Hastings to the Court of Directors, in which the following passage occurs :

" The great work achieved by your arms ought to be followed by a peace, of which you will be solicitous to avail yourselves as the fortunate opportunity for disseminating instruction and morals among immense communities, lamentably deficient in the conception of social principles and duties. A vast field for the amelioration of man lies before us."

This field the British administrators commenced with zeal to till. They uprooted many ancient institutions, some of which were admittedly in a semi-ruinous condition, and substituted improvisations of their own, which, if well intended, were not seldom mistaken. But above all, they sowed a new and strange seed—that of Western education, concerning the fruits of which they prophesied with pathetic faith. To quote Elphinstone once more :

" It is now well understood that in all countries the happiness of the poor depends in great measure on their education. It is by means of it alone that they can acquire those habits of prudence and self-respect from which all other good qualities spring ; and if there is a country where such habits are required, it is this. We have all often heard of the ills of early marriages and overflowing population ; of the savings of a life squandered on some one occasion of festivity ; of the helplessness of the rayats which renders them a prey to moneylenders ; of their indifference to good clothes and houses, which has been urged on some occasions as an argument against lowering the public demands on them ; and finally, of the vanity of all laws to protect them where no individual can be found who has spirit enough to take advantage of those which acted in their favour. There is but one remedy for all this, which is education."

Unfortunately for the hopes of the prophets, this passage remains no less true to-day than when it was penned, one hundred and fourteen years ago. Indeed, it might have been " lifted " textually from the leader columns of an Indian-owned newspaper of 1938. But if the system of Western education introduced by the British has done little to change the age-old social customs and mental outlook of the Indian peasant, it has, as we shall see subsequently, exerted dynamic influence upon the Indian intellectual.

The well-intentioned efforts of the Company to " disseminate instruction and morals " were handicapped by a general contempt, only partly mitigated by the enthusiasm of exceptional individuals, for indigenous learning and for the institutions which imparted it. The cultural background of India was so different from that of the Western conquerors that in their view it was little better than barbarism. Even to-day this attitude has not quite disappeared ; and so lately as 1917 a distinguished man of letters, the late William Archer, could arrive at the conclusion that India was really a " barbarous " country. And although the Company's servants in the early nineteenth century included notable scholars, who began to reveal to the Western world something of the treasures of Hindu and Muslim literature and learning, there was a disposition to regard these things, not as the basis of a culture still living and vital, but as the strange and interesting relics of a civilization which, if not wholly dead, was destined rapidly to be superseded by the only true learning—that of the West.

For some time controversy raged between those officers of the Company who desired to encourage the study of Indian classical languages as a means of education and those who considered that anything other than Western learning, conveyed in a Western language, was a waste of time. The early tradition of the Company, from the days of Warren Hastings, favoured the former alternative ; and for some years Western books were translated into these languages. But their association with a non-Western cultural outlook, their position as the vehicle of religious teaching which was stigmatized as "heathen" by the earnest Christians of the day, and the mythological character of much of the instruction to be found in them, combined to defeat the efforts of those who wished to use them as a means of imparting Western education.

The scornful rhetoric of Macaulay settled the dispute for the moment ; it was, he wrote, only a question "whether, when we can patronise sound philosophy and true history, we shall countenance, at the public expense, medical doctrines which would disgrace an English farrier ; astronomy which would move laughter in girls at an English boarding school ; history abounding in kings thirty feet high and reigns thirty thousand years long ; and geography made of seas of treacle and seas of butter." It seems strange that Macaulay failed to perceive that similar strictures might, with equal justice, be applied to certain passages in the Old Testament, and indeed to the sacred books of many religions ; and in fact afford very slender grounds upon which to condemn great historic cultures. But the effect of his interposition was decisive. While the schools and colleges maintained by the Company for Oriental learning were continued, they became the resort of specialists. Education in Western subjects, conveyed in the English language, henceforward received the full support of the administration.

There is no doubt that the motives of the British in arriving at this decision were mainly disinterested. There were not wanting those who advised them that the introduction of Western ideas of politics and ethics among the governed would inevitably make the task of the governors less easy. On the other hand, there were those who urged that great convenience and economy would result from the creation of a class literate in English for employment in the subordinate ranks of the Company's services. But a study of the official papers leaves us with a conviction that the profoundly important decision to make English the medium of education was taken because it was considered to be in the larger interests of the Indians themselves. Indeed, the probability that access to Western thought would lead to a demand for Parliamentary institutions was foreseen and welcomed by many distinguished men, including Macaulay himself.

The theory underlying the plan actually adopted was this. It was assumed that when once the literate classes had been educated in English, Western learning, of which English was the medium, would gradually "filter down" to the masses. Eventually, every one would be educated, every one would be westernized, and—as a result—every one would become a Christian. This theory ignored two important realities of the Indian situation. In the first place, the influence of the caste system interposed an effective barrier between the classes traditionally concerned with learning, and the masses of the population ; so that until political developments within very recent years convinced the intelligentsia of the necessity of educating the masses to take part in politics, they passed on to them nothing of the new learning.

In the second place, the literate classes acquired English as in former times they had acquired Persian and doubtless other languages—for the purpose primarily of taking service with those who for the moment governed the country, and to whom the language was familiar. The mere fact of this acquisition did not make them less Indian, or attach them more closely in affection to their rulers ; their way of life and their habits of mind persisted alongside the Western learning which was at first a mere professional qualification, but which soon provided them with a logical argument for questioning the right of their rulers to rule at all. This remarkable reconciliation between a Western cultural outlook, to be used, as it were, in business hours, and a traditional way of life fundamentally opposed to Western ideas, was encouraged by the decision of the Government to give appointments by preference to English-educated Indians ; and was greatly facilitated by the domestic conservatism resulting from the practice, common to the literate classes of Hindus and Muslims alike, of secluding women from the influence of everything outside the home.

To begin with, there were not wanting those who took up the Western learning with the zeal of the newly-converted, and endeavoured to westernize themselves completely ; not merely in culture, but in ways of life. To do this entailed a complete break with the existing social structure, and the formation of fresh groups ; only so could the reformers find bridegrooms for their daughters and brides for their sons. Some of these groups were Christian ; for Christian missionaries were pioneers in the field of Western education. They laboured hard in translation ; they were among the first to introduce printing into India. Their influence spread far beyond the circle of their converts. They encouraged Western political ideas. They fostered a demand for Western education which was among the causes influencing the Company to supply it. They greatly stimulated the use of Bengali as a literary medium ; indeed, the growth of modern Bengali literature—a brilliant example to the rest of India—derives from the seed they sowed. Others of these groups were Deistic, such as the community known as Brahmo Samaj, formed by the distinguished scholar, Ram Mohan Roy, one of the earliest and most notable Indian advocates of Western education.

In general, the enthusiastic supporters of the new learning were severely critical both of Hinduism and of Islam. The orthodox retaliated ; and the Muslims, with their clear-cut creed which admits of little compromise, began to shun Western education as impious. The religious significance which the Arabic language possesses for them, and the place which Persian has always held among cultured Indian Muslims as the medium of polished intercourse, combined to make the acquisition of English difficult for them, and to discourage them from competing with the Hindus in the race for Western learning. This has reacted seriously upon their position in modern India ; and the effects are plain, even to-day.

The facilities for Western education provided in increasing measure by the Company, by missionary enterprise, and by private initiative, were engrossed by the Hindu literate classes. Vernacular education was neglected for a long period ; and the little village schools which still existed in many parts of India fell into decay. They were mainly associated with religion ; it was the temple Brahmin or the Mulla who gave simple instruction, almost entirely of an oral type. They had filled a real need ; and many a great Indian scholar must have laid the foundations of his learning in such

humble surroundings. But as they were not encouraged
or regularised, and constituted no link with the Western
education now becoming fashionable, they were for-
saken by the literate classes and gradually abandoned
by the people. As a result, Indian education gradually
became as top-heavy as we see it to-day ; literacy is
very low—only 95 per 1,000—for the country as a
whole. On the other hand the percentage of the population (of course, confined to the literate classes) attending secondary schools and universities is remarkably high.

The disadvantage attending this disproportionate development did not remain unnoticed for very long ; and
in 1854, as a result of a Parliamentary investigation into
Indian education, a well-thought-out plan was pressed
upon the Company by Sir Charles Wood. A complete
structure was devised, stretching from the primary school
to the university ; and much stress was laid upon the
necessity for vernacular education and the education of
women. The principles of the Wood despatch stand as
a model even to-day. But the results of such earnest
effort have been on the whole disappointing. The scale
of the problem has been too vast ; there has never been
money enough to tackle it thoroughly ; there has been
an irresistible temptation to allot the available funds to
the classes which have clamoured for education rather
than to embark upon the seemingly hopeless task of
thrusting education upon the masses who do not desire
it, and—possessing as they do the background of a
traditional culture orally transmitted—seem to feel little
need for it. Of late years, particularly since the control
of education has passed to Indian ministers in the provincial governments, great efforts have been made to
extend primary education, even by compulsion, in rural

as well as urban areas ; but the difficulties encountered through paucity of funds and lack of effective demand make progress slow.

It is an astonishing testimony to the strength and vitality of the caste system that it should have turned even so alien a force as Western education into a means of emphasizing the traditional distinction which it imposes between the literate and the unlettered classes. Western education was introduced by the British in the confident hope that it would lead to the "enlightenment" of the whole of India along Western lines. It has done nothing of the kind ; the probability is that it will never do so. What it has done is to bring into being an Indian intelligentsia, no longer confined to certain localities, but diffused all over the country, who themselves have created or adopted ideals common to them all. And the central core of these ideals is to make India less English and more Indian.

During the first half of the nineteenth century these consequences were hidden, to be revealed only within living memory. The promotion of Western education was eagerly pursued ; and as part of the general policy of government, *sati*, or the burning of widows on the husband's funeral pyre, was prohibited ; and the ancient secret society of the Thags, who committed treacherous ritual murders on unsuspecting travellers, was suppressed. The organization of the judiciary was improved. New regulations were introduced, which the law-courts enforced with unfailing certainty. The collection of the land revenue was placed upon a definite basis by an inquiry which in many parts of the country necessitated a field-to-field investigation. The electric telegraph was introduced ; road construction was taken up in right earnest ; the first stretches of railway were laid ; the irrigation engineers were fairly launched upon their beneficent labour, which in our own time has attained such astonishing proportions. In all this activity the state itself took the lead ; and for perhaps the first time in its history, the territory now known as British India came to experience the all-pervading influence of a strong centralized government, whose arm was long enough to extend to the remotest village, and whose activities, veiled in mystery to many of those who were the objects of them, impinged more and more upon the life of the ordinary man.

The Indian masses, whose folk-memory goes back so far, had seen activities similar in nature, if not perhaps in pervasiveness, undertaken by many other conquerors. New brooms, they were well aware, swept clean. This energy would doubtless not endure ; and life would at length resume its traditional tenor. Such an expectation was doomed to be disappointed. The British zeal was unabating ; for every year brought out fresh and vigorous men to take the place of those of whom the Indian climate and the Indian conditions were taking toll. The cutting-edge of the mind of these new masters never grew blunt ; their aims were never abandoned ; secure and confident, they worked with the relentless persistence of some natural law. Like other conquerors, they had settled down as a dominant caste. But it was a caste which could not be assimilated into the social structure ; for it was a caste which did not make its home in the country. The original asperities of intercourse were not softened by time and circumstance ; the strange ideas were not mellowed into harmony with Indian conditions; the Western culture of the Western invaders could neither be absorbed nor evaded. By the time a century had passed since the battle of Plassey, a feeling of uneasiness had developed in many parts of the country.

Of this uneasiness the majority of the servants of the Company took little heed. England was in the heyday of that long peace which endured from Waterloo to the Crimea. It was the era which witnessed the abolition of slavery, Catholic emancipation, the Reform Act. Public opinion had infinite faith in the perfectability of men ; good intentions carried out with firm benevolence could effect miracles. Parliament was much concerned with the well-being of India ; it laid down in specific terms that Indians should not be debarred from official positions on ground of race ; that the interests of " the native subjects " were in all cases to take precedence over those of Europeans. Could any one doubt, when our intentions were so good and our policy so enlightened, that India was being bound to Britain by ever-strengthening bonds of gratitude and goodwill ?

But in effect a violent reaction occurred, which history records as the Indian Mutiny. Concerning its causes, there is an extensive literature, but the main facts are plain. The all-pervading energy of the Government had offended many powerful interests ; the operation of the new laws enabling mortgaged land to be sold had ruined numbers of landowners. Orthodox Hindus and Muslims believed that the unprecedented educational activity following the Wood despatch represented an organized attack on religion. Railways were believed to be a device to break down caste—a consequence which certain missionaries were so unguarded as to prophesy. Enactments permitting a convert to Christianity to retain his share in the property of the joint family, and allowing

98

the re-marriage of Hindu widows, were cited as evidence of Government's design of wholesale proselytization. Again, the Muslim community was particularly discontented. The Empire of Delhi, still pursuing a shadowy existence, remained to remind them of the once-dominant position they had now lost. Traditionally disinclined to adopt the new Western learning, deprived by the British peace of the power of asserting themselves by arms, and losing to the better-educated Hindus their old share of official appointments, it is little wonder that the Muslims were for the most part utterly hostile. Further, Lord Dalhousie's assertion of his claim to annex Indian states whose origin did not ante-date British rule, if direct heirs failed to the dynasties, drove a certain number of influential people to desperation. Military checks on the frontier and in the Sikh wars had destroyed the old legend of the invulnerability of British power.

Materials were thus at hand for a conflagration, which any spark might start. It is quite possible that the tension might have subsided had there not existed an organized body of men who shared the general feeling of discontent and had power to put their sentiments into operation— the Bengal Army. The incident of the greased cartridges provided the spark, and the combustible material blazed up. The momentary paucity of British troops, and the failure of many regimental officers to take action with the necessary promptitude, allowed the insurrection to spread. As a contemporary Indian observer remarked : " One knave led astray nine fools and then told them they had gone too far to draw back."

From a military point of view, the Mutiny was from the first hopeless. Many of the regiments even of the Bengal Army—the only one disaffected—remained loyal to their officers. The newly-embodied Punjab held firmly to the British. The Indian states, with insignificant exceptions, supported us promptly and effectively in accordance with their treaty pledges. Above all, sea power promptly exerted its overwhelming might, and regiment after regiment of British troops poured into the country. Among the mutineers there was no common aim, little concerted effort, much division. Racial bitterness was inflamed, and as is commonly the case, those who suffered from the reprisals of both sides were often completely innocent of all offence. The masses of the population were unmoved, seldom displaying hostility and often manifesting great kindness to helpless European fugitives. When the local landlord was in sympathy with the mutineers, his tenants generally took their cue from him. But large numbers of Europeans owed their lives to the chivalrous kindness of both prince and peasant.

The Mutiny marks a dividing line in the history of British rule. The immediate consequence, as must always be the case when the weaker of two parties resorts to violence, was to produce embittered relations and some symptoms of a new ruthless exercise of power. Both Britain and India owe much to the wisdom of the then Governor-General, Lord Canning, who firmly maintained that when once the outbreak was over " deliberate justice and calm reason " must resume their sway. But for him the newly-opened gulf between British and Indians might well have proved impassable. As it was, the traditions of the Mutiny have exerted a most sinister influence upon the relations between the races.

The sufferings inflicted upon English women and children were for many years remembered with bitterness ; and the fact that the number of English women coming to India was greatly augmented in the period which followed, owing to the improvement of sea-communications, added a further complication. For their presence made the British community even more self-contained than before ; served to enhance racial feeling by necessitating additional security precautions ; and made social intercourse with Indians—whose women were mostly in seclusion—so one-sided as to be difficult. The British community drew itself further apart than before ; the old easy, confident, if patronizing, intercourse with their subjects was replaced by more formal relations. The British began to think less of the virtues of zeal and enthusiasm, more of those of caution and prudence. They were still animated by a lofty conception of their duties, but they henceforth thought also of the difficulties to which their position as rulers exposed them. Their responsibilities to the peoples of India were now tempered by the realization that " the Eastern Empire must be held."

From this time forward there was much hesitation in interfering with customs which could be represented as bound up with religion, and the pace of social reform slowed down. The old " missionary spirit " which had inspired the early administrators gave place to the con-scientious routine of the careful official. The knowledge that so much fervour and such excellent intentions had not sufficed to win the hearts of the bulk of their subjects, came as a cruel shock to many Englishmen. During the decades that followed the Mutiny there was a tendency to concentrate, as it were, upon the material advancement of the country, rather than upon the task of moral or spiritual inspiration. Roads, bridges, canals, hospitals,

railways, the maintenance of peace, the administration
of justice, the organization of famine relief, the encouragement of productive agriculture—these were tangible and
safe things, obviously beneficent, obviously worth doing.
The intangibles, such as the development of Indian
nationality or the encouragement of political integration,
must be left to themselves. They had been plainly shown
to be beyond the ken even of the most disinterested and
benevolent administration. For this reason the post-
Mutiny officials, though they devoted themselves to their
work as conscientiously as ever, though they toiled un-
sparingly for the benefit of the people over whom they
ruled, indulged in few hopes and fewer speculations
concerning the future of India or of the Indo-British
connection. The day's work more than sufficed for the
day ; no doubt the future could look after itself.

This limitation of outlook, this concentration upon
obvious tasks, was accentuated by the transfer, in 1858, of
the governance of India from the Company to the Crown.
The Company had been for so long under the effective
control of the Cabinet that the practical consequences of
the change were not very marked, except in two par-
ticulars. In the first place there then began that intimate
tie between the Sovereign and the Princes and peoples of
India which has been among the most gracious elements
in the Indo-British connection. The personal devotion
manifested towards the Throne by many Indians who
disapprove of certain features of the British administration
of India, has played a large part in such crises as the outbreak of the war of 1914–18. The second consequence
was not so happy. While the Company existed the
charter had to be renewed periodically. Each renewal
entailed a meticulous examination of the affairs of India

by Parliament ; a new declaration, sometimes involving a re-orientation, of British policy ; and an effective control over the lines of advance henceforth to be followed. With the disappearance of the Company the occasions for this examination ceased. The destinies of India were committed, with a confidence that was by no means unmerited, to administrators on the spot. In consequence, from 1858 until 1917 no clear-cut policy for the future relationship between Britain and India was laid down. Looking back over the course of events, it is difficult to escape the conclusion that if parliamentary control over India had been exercised as fully and effectively after 1858 as before that date, the progress of the country towards self-government would have proceeded with far less friction than it has done.

CHAPTER VI

THE RISE OF INDIAN NATIONALISM

THE establishment of British rule over a large portion of India, and the extension of British peace throughout the entire country, together ensured the conditions in which the spirit of nationalism could grow. This growth commenced with the spread of Western education among the literate classes ; and although the spirit is no longer confined wholly to these classes, they constitute even to-day its principal vehicle.

During the period which has elapsed since the Mutiny, the Muslims have followed, though somewhat tardily, in the wake of the Hindus. Muslim leaders, inspired by the genius of some exceptional men, notably Sir Syed Ahmad Khan, realized that it was suicidal for the community to turn its back upon Western learning ; and there have grown up institutions like the Aligarh University, the Islamia College at Peshawar, and the Osmania University at Hyderabad, which enable young Muhammadans to acquire the culture of Europe in harmonious conformity with the dictates of their faith. Educated Muslims have succeeded in organizing themselves in an all-India body, the Muslim League, corresponding to the dominantly Hindu organization—which also includes Muslim membership—of the Indian National Congress. In an earlier chapter we have noticed the communal tension resulting from the determination on either side to insist upon the importance of communal claims ; but we have also seen that this tension does not prevent Hindus and Muslims from joining in concerted political agitation against the British. It is with the inception and progress of the spirit inspiring this agitation that we are here concerned.

We must picture, then, the rapid and cumulative growth during the last century in many parts of India, but principally in the larger towns, of a middle class educated in English. To begin with, English learning was largely a professional qualification, useful for Government service, for commerce, for legal work, and for journalism. But the mastery of the language led insensibly to mastery of the literature—a result facilitated by the predominantly literary character of the type of education in vogue ; and with the literature came a spate of new ideas. English history taught the lesson of the gradual acquisition of popular liberties, English political thought as expressed by Burke and Mill reinforced the lesson. Educated Indians, essentially keen intellectually, and readily stirred to enthusiasm, perceived a new revelation. Constitutional maxims, evolved in very special circumstances, were regarded as of universal application ; and political discussion, which became increasingly popular with the growth of English as a *lingua franca* and of a vigorous, only spasmodically controlled English and vernacular Press, assumed the vocabulary successively of liberalism, of radicalism, and of democracy.

The academic and speculative character which from the early days of British rule has distinguished Indian thought and speech upon political questions, has been somewhat rigorously condemned by many English observers. These point out that Indian claims to self-government frequently take too much for granted, proceeding upon the assumption that external peace and internal security are of the natural order of things ; that an elaborate bureaucratic machine will run itself in a fool-proof manner ; that the delicate balance of rights and interests prevailing in a sectionally-organized country can be maintained without the exercise of any particular skill.

There is some force in these criticisms ; but the manner in which the Indian mind deals with problems, whether of politics or of ethics, differs fundamentally, as we noticed in the first chapter, from the Western methods of approach. When once the literate class became convinced, from its study of British constitutional principles, that these principles formed a sound basis for political organization, it tended to assume their inherent universal validity, without regard to the particular circumstances obtaining in a small insular country from which they had taken their rise. With the principles of government by discussion and of majority decision the literate caste was well acquainted. Such methods had been practised from time immemorial within the joint family, the village community, and the caste-gathering. That these principles had never been extended to the nation-wide state was perfectly true ; but then the nation-wide state had not previously existed. Further, were not the inhabitants of British India now British subjects ? And as British subjects, was it not their natural right to take part in the government of their own country ?

Such were the questions which the educated Indians in many parts of India were already posing to themselves in the middle of the last century. It was only a question of time before the increasing ease of communications and the tendency of the whole country to draw together into an economic unit enabled the Western-educated classes of many different races and languages to realize a new unity of outlook, a new community of interest, and a new facility, through the medium of the English language, for the interchange of ideas.

In origin, this incipient spirit of nationalism was by no means hostile to British rule, for it was animated by a firm faith in the excellence of British institutions. Indeed, it was a guiding principle with the early Nationalist leaders that Britain would assuredly confer self-government upon India as soon as Indians had shown themselves worthy of the gift. For a good many years, accordingly, the efforts of the educated classes were limited to the aim of securing for themselves a share in the higher administrative posts. By this means they hoped, as time went on, to secure control of the administrative machine. India would then be governed by Indians, and all would be well.

But before long this simple plan was found to be inadequate, and for several reasons. In the first place, it was extremely difficult for Indians to enter the higher ranks of the administration in any considerable numbers ; for this entailed an expensive and arduous exile in England, where alone the qualifying examinations were held. Next, even when a few Indians did enter the Indian Civil Service, they were not welcomed by their British colleagues as equals—they were still treated as Indians. For such treatment there was no doubt a logical defence, in that, with rare exceptions, even the English-educated Indian still retained his own cultural background, his own habits of life, and his own traditional outlook on such matters as the status of women. And these factors held good, of course, in far greater degree, of the mass of Indians who from the first occupied the subordinate posts.

But the effects of this racial exclusiveness were very marked, and largely account for the contrast between conditions to-day in British India and those which are to be found in the Dutch and French possessions in the East. Both Dutch and French have proceeded on the assumption that when one of their oriental subjects enters the administrative cadre he forthwith qualifies as a member of the ruling race. Even mixed marriages are regarded with an indulgent eye in such circumstances. In India the British have never been able to bring themselves to take this view ; with the result that the members of the educated classes who have entered Government service, although performing their duties with zeal, ability, and conscientiousness, have never been among the staunch supporters of British rule, and have frequently been known as its severest critics. This has been a source of weakness to the administration at times when the mind of political India has been deeply stirred—for example, during the non-co-operation campaign under Mr. Gandhi's leadership.

The rigidity of the British caste has often been re-marked by impartial observers, who have not failed to perceive its disastrous effects in accentuating racial feeling. Unfortunately, this rigidity was particularly directed against the Western-educated Indians, who alone aspired to be accepted by the British as equals. With other classes of the population the same trouble did not arise. The orthodox Hindus regarded the British as untouchable, if masterful, barbarians, disliking both them and their learning. The labouring classes, in the advancement of whose material welfare the British found their chosen sphere of work, were too remote in status and outlook to be treated with anything but paternal control, animated by real affection and kindness. It is with the Western-educated Indian that friction has occurred. This was in the nature of things to some extent inevitable, for the Western-educated Indian aspired to replace the British. But the real bitterness centres round the fact that the majority of British administrators have never really liked him. He has been, as it were, driven further than necessary along the path of opposition ; his political antagonisms have been sharpened by his treatment as an inferior. Thus spurred on, he has frequently thrown himself with relish into the task of destructive criticism, which was for long the only outlet for his feelings.

From early days there were not wanting those who pointed out that in the suggestion that the Indianization of the Administrative Services would lead to self-government for India there was a serious confusion of thought. The classes who could alone take the place of the British administrators represented a small oligarchy of learning. They were separated by a traditional gulf from the masses of the people. By what means, then, could they reconcile their employment of the language of democracy with the position which would result from the achievement of their ambitions ? It is doubtful whether this criticism has ever made much appeal to the educated classes. The specialization of function resulting from the caste system naturally inclined them to assume that the task of administration would fall within their own sphere, with which members of other castes, including the masses, would have no desire to meddle. Within this sphere, which they themselves would engross, affairs would naturally be determined, as affairs of importance to the castes always had been determined, by discussion and by the will of the majority. Was not this procedure sufficiently " democratic " to harmonize with Western principles ? Surely nothing more could be wanted ? The mere fact that this British importation—the supreme centralized state—was something new in India hardly affected the issue. They had been the instruments, since time immemorial, of many different types of administration. At the same time, they were shrewd enough to know that this objection, if allowed to remain unanswered, would prejudice their claims with public opinion in England.

Thus, partly on account of resentment at the exclusiveness of the British, who refused to accept them as equals even when they rose to equal rank ; partly from a desire to broaden the basis of their claim to power ; and partly from an increasing enthusiasm for the parliamentary principle of government, the educated classes began to associate an aspiration to political control of the administration with their earlier claim to participate in administrative activities. For some time there was much uncertainty as how best to achieve this aim. It was suggested that the Indian provinces should be represented in the House of Commons. It was also suggested that India should have a parliament of its own. In the end the latter idea prevailed, fostered doubtless by the realization that legislatures already existed in India which could presumably be adapted to the purpose now formulated.

The development of these Indian legislatures provides, over a very short period, an interesting example of that gradual specialization of function which lies at the root of parliamentary institutions.

From its earliest days the East India Company had possessed powers of legislation conferred by Queen Elizabeth's charter, authorizing it to make " laws, constitutions, orders and ordinances " for the good government of its affairs. Of these regulations not a trace remains ; but we may conjecture that they were of the nature of executive orders, applicable only to the Company's employees. The authority to make them is omitted from the charters of the time of William III. and Mary. But in 1726 there was an important step forward ; the Governors-in-Council, established as we saw in an earlier chapter, in the three presidencies, were authorized by Parliament to make laws for the inhabitants of the Company's territories.

This event is of great significance, for it means that the original source of law-making authority in India was a parliamentary grant. Hence arose a curious constitutional anomaly which, right up to our own time, has puzzled successive generations of British statesmen. For how was it possible to reconcile the growing claim of the Nationalists that the executive should be controlled by the legislature with the hard constitutional fact that the legal sources of executive and legislative authority alike were to be found, not in India, but in Britain ?

The immediate consequence of Parliament's interposition into Indian affairs was to produce a strong tendency towards centralization, further reinforcing the conception of the new centralized state which the British were creating in India. The Regulating Act of 1773 set the Governor-General and Council of Bengal over the presidencies of Madras and Bombay ; and in a country less diverse than India, legislative uniformity would soon have developed. But while executive centralization was realized comparatively early, the difference in local conditions enabled all three presidencies to remain independent legislative units until 1833. The Charter Act of that year completed the legislative, as well as the executive, centralization of British India by depriving the governments of Madras and Bombay of all power of legislation, and by laying down the principle that, in the last resort, the supreme authority in every branch of statal activity must remain with the Government of India. Only within the last twenty years has this principle been substantially modified.

Until the passing of the Act of 1833, the law-making activities of the three presidencies had been carried on by purely executive action. But we can now discern the first traces of the evolution of a true legislative function, differing in method from the ordinary executive activities of the Government. A special Law Member, whose duties were confined to legislative matters, was added to the Council of the Governor-General. Here again is a significant landmark, which represents the beginning of that gradual differentiation of the legislative from the executive lying at the root of democratic development in India.

In 1853 occurred the last of those grand inquisitions to which Parliament was periodically, if reluctantly, driven by the necessity of renewing the Company's charter. Opportunity was taken to make a concession to administrative convenience which contained the germs of an important constitutional principle. It had been found in practice that the local legislative requirements of the subordinate governments could not be satisfied unless local representatives were present to supply detailed information. Accordingly, the Governor - General's Council in its legislative capacity was strengthened by the inclusion of nominees of the governments of Madras, Bengal, Bombay, and Agra, as well as of two judges of the Supreme Court. At the same time, significant changes in procedure occurred. Oral discussion replaced written minutes ; Bills were referred to Select Committee instead of to the Law Member alone ; legislative business was transacted in public.

Lord Dalhousie, the Governor-General of the day, was largely responsible for these developments. He wrote in 1854 : " Our young Parliament is going on smoothly. It has given me a great deal of trouble to bring it into the world, and its sittings break up one day in the week for me, which is a serious affair ; but it is a vastly superior machine to the last, and will do a great deal of business."

Lord Dalhousie's description of the new legislative machine as a " young Parliament " was truer than he realized or indeed intended. Although the British in India constituted an essentially autocratic type of administration, even a handful of nominated officials could not shed their traditional habit of mind when they gathered round a table. Within a few years the " young Parliament " caused the executive grave concern. It demanded to be shown confidential correspondence between the President of the Board of Control and the Governor-General ; it questioned the validity of the law-making functions retained by the executive for the " non-regulation " provinces. Sir Charles Wood himself complained in the House of Commons that it was arrogating to itself the function of a " petty Parliament."

The executive determined to confine this " handful of legislators " strictly to law-making.

The Mutiny exercised a considerable influence upon the development of the Indian legislature, for it convinced the executive that to neglect Indian opinion was perilous. Obviously, therefore, it was necessary to ascertain what Indian opinion was. Steps were accordingly taken, cautious and tentative at first, to associate representatives of Indian opinion with the law - making functions of government. From this point of view the Indian Councils Act of 1861 is important, for it expanded the Central Legislature to make room for a new non-official element, both Indian and " European " (as the British in India rather curiously term themselves). Also, while the Governor-General's Legislative Council, thus augmented, could legislate for the whole of India, the local legislative councils, also strengthened with a non-official element, were again utilized to make laws for their own area, subject to the Governor-General's consent.

By degrees, as other administrative areas were brought into a uniform system, the number of local legislatures increased, so that the number of non-official "Europeans" and Indians associated with the work of legislation was correspondingly augmented. During this period the executive successfully limited these legislatures to the function of law-making ; they were not allowed to urge redress of grievances, to vote supplies, or to ask questions. But the non-official " Europeans "—for the most part business men and leaders of the British commercial community—did not take these unfamiliar limitations kindly ; and often showed a disposition to join hands with their Indian colleagues as against the British officials in pressing for an enlargement of the functions of the legislatures. After the reforms of 1892 this tendency became more marked ; and in 1894, when Lancashire interests forced the Government of India to put countervailing excise duties upon Indian cotton manufactures (see below, page 157), the British business men in the legislatures protested no less stoutly than their Indian colleagues. The debt which Indian political life owes to the non-official Briton has never been adequately recognized ; but it is a very real one.

The official view that the new legislative bodies were merely governmental committees for law-making, and were in no sense embryo representative institutions, was constitutionally correct ; for the legislative authority of the Government of India was derived, not from the people of India, but from parliamentary grant. It was thus to Parliament, and not to the people of India, that the Government, both in its executive and in its legislative function, was alike responsible. But it will readily be understood that the mere existence of these legislatures and their inclusion of a few nominated Indian members, stimulated among the Western-educated Indians the desire for parliamentary institutions, and strengthened their determination to control the administrative machine by converting these legislatures into parliaments. They either did not perceive, or did not attach importance to, the difficulty that the legal source of legislative power was not indigenous but alien. In any case, the line of advance that lay open was too obvious to be neglected.

In the two decades between 1870 and 1890 the old plan of obtaining self-government for India by the simple process of Indianizing the higher ranks of the administrative services was recognized as inadequate. A series of events widened the gulf already dividing the Western-educated classes from the British officials. The effort made by Lord Lytton to restrain the increasing licence of the vernacular Press ; the restriction placed upon the possession of firearms ; above all, perhaps, the agitation among non-official " Europeans " against the attempt of Lord Ripon (Viceroy, 1880–84) in the " Ilbert Bill " to put Indian I.C.S. magistrates upon the same footing, for the trial of " European " offenders, as their British colleagues—these convinced the educated classes that the British would never accept them as equals. Hence, while the claim of the educated classes to occupy the highest positions in the administrative cadre was not abandoned, the spokesmen of the growing nationalist sentiment realized that it must be supplemented by the further claim to control political development through command of the legislatures. The existing legislatures, owing to their limited functions, did not provide a suitable forum for the ventilation of nationalist claims. Therefore another, if necessarily unofficial, forum must be created.

It was in such circumstances that the Indian National Congress came into being in 1885, gradually attracting to itself other organizations started with a similar purpose. Its early success was due largely to the enthusiasm of A. O. Hume, a retired I.C.S. official, and to the steady support of a number of British business men and barristers. It took its stand upon two main principles—support of the connection between India and Britain ; and support of the claim of the educated classes to enjoy the advantage in their own country of British institutions. Thus while it became increasingly critical of the policy and action of the British ruling caste in India, it maintained close touch with England, labouring to convince

British public opinion that the claims of the educated classes deserved to be recognized.

During the first twenty years of its existence, the Indian National Congress held steadily to its aim of remodelling the structure of the Indian Government in such fashion as to bring it in harmony with the Western conception of a parliamentary system. It set up standing committees at all important centres ; and by degrees its organization covered the whole of British India. At first, it was regarded as harmless, or even commendable by the officials. But before long its criticisms were found increasingly embarrassing, for it concentrated its attack upon institutions and practices which were based rather upon administrative convenience than upon readily defensible principles. Thus its reiterated and closely reasoned demands for the expansion of the legislatures into representative institutions ; for the extension of the jury system ; for the appointment of Indians to the Privy Council ; for the expansion of technical education ; for simultaneous I.C.S. examinations in India and England ; for the modification of the Arms Act, the creation of Volunteer Corps, and the provision of Military Colleges ; for the removal of the salary of the Secretary of State for India from the Indian to the Home Estimates ; were the more inconvenient at the time on account of the inherent justification which made subsequent concession inevitable.

At this period of its development, both the aims and the methods of the Congress made a strong appeal to the traditional constitutionalism of the average Englishman ; and it is probable that more substantial concessions would have been made but for the danger which such a course was considered to involve. The British officials, then as more recently, tended to hold a low opinion of the executive capacity of the educated Indian, whom they regarded as better at talking about a thing than at doing it. They knew themselves to be accomplishing much for the material development of the country as well as for its peace and order ; they were genuinely apprehensive lest the interests of the masses should suffer if this work, now performed by a *corps d'élite* devoting every ounce of its skill, " nerve," and determination to the job, should fall into less competent hands.

It was this consideration which accounted for the comparative failure of the attempt made by Lord Ripon to institute a formal system of local self-government for India on the English model. The skill and experience of the British officials who presided over the Municipalities and District Boards overawed the elected members, whose influence was accordingly small. Men of local rank and substance soon became reluctant to offer themselves for election ; and in practice the British officials continued to administer local affairs much as before. This was the more regrettable because, as we have seen, India possesses a real tradition of local self-government in the shape of its own institutions. But the British could not bear to stand aside and see their work done less efficiently by some one else. It was thirty-five years before local self-government became a reality under Lord Chelmsford (Viceroy, 1916–21).

To understand the British attitude, it must be remembered that in this sphere, as in the higher branches of the administration, they looked upon themselves as the protectors of the masses, as against those who, under the cloak of a programme of political advance, designed to exploit them in the interests of a narrow caste oligarchy. Such a standpoint was the more tenable in view of the prevailingly Hindu—and indeed Brahminical—character of the Indian National Congress at this date. It was along this line that a case was found for resisting the nationalist claims ; but even so, concessions were made which before long altered the whole position.

A notable advance resulted from the initiative of Lord Dufferin (Viceroy, 1884–88), who was deeply exercised by the necessity of obtaining a more exact knowledge of the sentiments of the various sections of the community. He proposed that the non-official elements in the legislatures, central and local, should be chosen as far as possible by the principle of election. The suggestion was accepted in a modified form by the Home Government, and found expression in Lord Cross's Act of 1892. Nor was this the only triumph of Congress ideas ; for the legislatures were now given rights of interpellation and of discussing the Budget. The completeness of the breach with the official theory, so long firmly maintained, that the legislatures were mere consultative committees to advise the executive on law-making, was hardly realized at the time. An attempt was made to reconcile the political " responsiveness " of the executive to Indian opinion, as expressed in the legislatures, with its constitutional responsibility to Parliament, by the retention of an official majority which in the last resort enabled the will of the executive to prevail. It was a compromise typical of British trial-and-error methods. Its weakness was at once apparent to the more logically-minded Indians.

The closing years of the nineteenth century were a period of considerable uneasiness in India. The fall in the value of silver—India's traditional medium of hoarding ; the incidence of severe famine due to successive failures of the rains ; the coming on a large scale of bubonic plague necessitating sanitary measures at variance with many social prejudices, all combined to provide new and formidable ammunition to the critics of Government. They did more ; they lent strength to a movement, which had for some time been growing, of definite hostility to Britain and the British. We have already noticed that from the early days of the introduction of Western education there had existed an orthodox party which would have nothing to do with it, condemning it as unholy and subversive of the traditional culture of India. This party had for long remained politically obscure in comparison with the party advocating constitutional reform on Western lines, although it derived increasing strength from racial bitterness and from the slowness with which the " constitutionalists " won their concessions.

The orthodox party, as it may for the moment be called, had a definite ideology of its own ; voicing the superiority of the ancient Hindu culture, and deriving much impetus from the " back to the Vedas " movement associated with the Arya Samaj, and with such influential spiritual leaders as Swami Dayanand and Swami Vivekananda. To those Indians who were discouraged by the apparently irresistible power of the British, and the seeming impossibility of wresting from them any real control over the country, this party offered a message of pride and hopefulness. Whatever might be the material achievements of the West, Hinduism embodied a spiritual superiority of infinitely greater eternal value. Let Hinduism then rally its forces along the old orthodox lines against these barbarians from Europe ! Basing itself as it did upon traditional Hindu culture, the orthodox party made a strong appeal to the student class with their characteristic idealism ; to all who were disappointed in the struggle for success in life ; and—significant phenomenon—to the masses, who are moved by religion when they are deaf to politics. With this party was identified the formidable personality of Bal Gangadhar Tilak, who turned his organizing ability to the revival of the Maratha traditions of martial glory based on " defence of the cow and the Brahmin." He despised parliamentary methods of agitation ; he preached " direct action," and extolled patriotic self-sacrifice even when this took the form of political assassination.

For some time he was unable to make much headway among the Congress party, who disliked his methods, and considered his uncompromisingly Hindu ideology, which was already alarming the Muslims, a political blunder. But the discontent of the educated classes was greatly inflamed during the viceroyalty of Lord Curzon (1899–1905). He pursued with single-minded zeal the ideal of administrative efficiency, which in his view was largely identical with centralization and with the untrammelled operation of the executive over which he presided so brilliantly. He promoted many far-reaching policies designed for the benefit of the country as a whole ; but since modern means of communication now made the arm of the central government very long, an increasing number of people felt themselves interfered with, disturbed, and shaken out of their ancient ways. He cherished, almost as an article of faith, his conviction of the superiority of Englishmen over Indians; he disliked political changes ; and he refused to see in the nationalist movement anything except the personal ambitions of a handful of men striving for place and power. It was not only that he opposed Indian opinion as expressed in the Press and from the platform—he ignored it altogether. His remodelling of the Calcutta Corporation, his drastic reduction of the popular element in the control of universities, and, above all, his administrative partition of Bengal—at the time the stronghold of nationalist sentiment—combined to galvanize the educated classes into a fury of impotent opposition.

In the general turmoil the orthodox party gathered force ; and its policy of " direct action " found expression in such movements as the boycott of British goods, mass agitation among the student-community, anarchist conspiracies, and political assassination. The tension between the British administration and the educated classes was much increased by these activities, while the victory of Japan over Russia—represented as a triumph of the East over the West—encouraged many Indian Nationalists to hope that Britain herself was not, in the last resort, invincible. Congress, although it refused to adopt Tilak's policy and methods, began to couch its demands in more peremptory tones. It was brilliantly led by such statesmen as G. K. Gokhale and Pherozeshah Mehta, and in contrast to the orthodox party began to exercise a great influence upon many British statesmen who were concerned at the condition of Indian affairs.

The Liberal Government of the day accordingly made a real effort to " rally the moderates," not without success. The Muslims, who were really alarmed by the political activities of the Hindus, and had established their own League in 1906, asked for and obtained assurances that in the political changes then under consideration their particular interests should be safeguarded by separate electorates. The reforms of 1909 made a number of concessions to Congress feeling. Indians were admitted into the Executive Council of the Governor-General and into the Council of the Secretary of State for India. The electoral principle was considerably extended in the constitution of the legislatures central and local, but was cautiously based upon a narrow franchise and the separate representation of different classes and communities.

The "moderates" were triumphant; and their success was sealed by the revocation, in 1911, of the partition of Bengal; a step which further alarmed the Muslims, who had constituted an overwhelming majority in the new province which now disappeared.

The orthodox party began to split up. The old conservative religious element remained strongly opposed to Western ways, and interested itself less and less in party politics. It was stoutly anti-Muslim as well as anti-British. But a new element now emerged, which was more militant. Its members may henceforth properly be termed the party of the Left, since they were increasingly influenced by the desire to learn what the West could teach regarding the technique of violence, and were no longer animated by purely Indian ideology. The Left were for the time driven into the political wilderness.

But while on the one hand the influence of the educated classes in the legislatures was enormously enhanced, and the prestige of the "moderate" party in control of Congress greatly increased, nothing was done to remedy the inherent contradiction in principle which we have already noticed. The executive was not—could not be, consistently with constitutional propriety—responsible to the legislature ; but was expected to be " responsive " to its opinions. Lord Morley himself was determined to confine the Indian legislatures to advisory functions. As he said in the House of Lords :

" If I were attempting to set up a parliamentary system in India, or if it could be said that this chapter of reforms led directly or necessarily up to the establishment of a parliamentary system in India, I, for one, would have nothing at all to do with it."

In little more than ten years it was found necessary to bring the constitutional basis of the Indian legislatures more closely in harmony with the realities of the situation. But for the war of 1914–18, it is doubtful whether the Morley-Minto constitution would have lasted as long as it did. The fundamental contradiction upon which it was based soon became apparent. Already non-official majorities in certain provinces were refusing to pass legislation which the executive deemed essential ; and the discretionary authority of the Governor-General had to be invoked to remedy the situation.

CHAPTER VII

THE NEW ERA IN POLITICS

THE outbreak of the war served to stimulate the spirit of Indian Nationalism in a variety of ways. The ideals proclaimed by the Allies convinced the educated classes that Britain could no longer refuse them their claims. They gave us support which, considering their relations with the administration, can only be termed surprisingly generous. They were not, of course, fighting men ; and there was a tendency for this reason to underestimate the value of their aid. This was unfair to them. During the early critical months of the war, they not only refrained from embarrassing the administration—which they could readily have done—but they eagerly sought opportunities, often short-sightedly denied them, of co-operating in every way they could. India's part in the war evoked enthusiasm in England, and somewhat lavish promises were made in gratitude. But the struggle dragged on ; the zeal of the educated classes was little utilized and began to flag ; nothing was done for India, while there was much talk of Imperial Federation and of the new position which the Dominions would occupy in relation to the Mother Country. Now India had its own grievances against the Dominions, whose governments sometimes treat Indian settlers in a fashion which offends Indian pride ; and accordingly the educated classes were greatly alarmed by the thought that India might, as a result of Imperial reconstruction, be subordinated in some degree to the Dominions as well as to Britain.

Political agitation therefore recommenced ; and the late Mrs. Besant, who joined the Congress in 1914, saw the opportunity to unite the Moderates with the Left upon a common platform of " Home Rule for India." By adroit manœuvres she brought about a coalition, and —greater triumph still—the Muslim League supported her campaign. Like Tilak, she did not confine her activities to the educated classes, and used all her remarkable ability to arouse the masses to political consciousness. She attained considerable success. The Government of India was embarrassed, and interned her. Political tension grew. The Moderate party, weakened by the death of brilliant leaders, was discredited ; and the Left captured the Congress machinery.

Very fortunately the seriousness of the Indian situation now attracted real attention in Britain ; more fortunately still, fresh minds were brought to bear upon it. An entire re-orientation of British policy followed. The consequence was the historic declaration of August 1917. Mr. E. S. Montagu stated in the House of Commons :

" The policy of His Majesty's Government, with which the Government of India are in complete accord, is that of the increasing association of Indians in every branch of the administration, and the gradual development of self-governing institutions, with a view to the progressive realization of responsible government in India as an integral part of the British Empire."

He proceeded to explain that substantial steps in this direction were to be taken immediately, and that he was himself going to India to explore the situation ; but that progress could only be achieved by stages ; and that the Home and the Indian Governments must be judges of the time and the manner of each advance.

Unfortunately, before expression could be given to the new policy, the political atmosphere in India had lamentably deteriorated. The educated classes thought they detected, with the victory of the Allies, a hardening of the British attitude towards their aspirations. The Muslims were profoundly disturbed by the helplessness of Turkey. Bad monsoons, rising prices, and a frightful influenza epidemic which slew nearly seven million people, caused the mass of the population in many parts of India to become restless and discontented. The ill-timed introduction of legislative measures intended to restrain anarchic crime, and designed to confer upon the executive wide discretionary powers, infuriated political leaders of all shades, who complained that they were treated to repression where they had expected emancipation.

Mr. Gandhi, that strange and enigmatic figure, so typical of the fundamentally " other-worldly " background of Indian culture, now began to assume high political significance. He had won in South Africa a great reputation as a protector of his countrymen from injustice, and had become convinced of the efficacy of organized passive resistance as a means of subduing for righteous ends even the most powerful administrations. His obvious sincerity, austere life, and unfaltering moral courage made a strong appeal to the idealism of youth ; while his confidence in his own methods—essentially compatible with Hindu traditional ideas—brought a message of hope to those who feared that the British

Government was too strong to yield to any pressure which Indians might bring upon it. By doing what Tilak could never have brought himself to do—by espousing the cause of the alarmed and aggrieved Muslims —Mr. Gandhi found himself at the head of a temporarily united opposition, consisting of elements ordinarily incompatible, prepared to support him in a " nation-wide campaign." He captured the entire Congress organization, and headed a movement of passive resistance and " non-co-operation." Unfortunately this degenerated into widespread mob-violence, with loss of life on both sides. Repression was stern—in certain places, as at Amritsar, astonishingly pitiless. Racial passions were vividly inflamed. Once again an invader thought he saw an opportunity to exploit India's domestic troubles. But British arms were still strong, and the Afghan Amir was quickly convinced of his mistake.

The Montagu - Chelmsford Reforms were thus launched in the least favourable circumstances that could well be imagined. This was unfortunate. Although very complicated in their details, full of checks and balances, and fundamentally tentative, the new constitutional arrangements embodied two principles of the highest importance. In the first place, they restored the traditional balance of the Indian polity by an effective demarcation of the sphere of provincial authority. Centralization was from henceforward to be balanced by decentralization, and an important field was allotted to local activity, always so vital to India's wellbeing. At the same time, the centre retained the task of co-ordination ; and in general was supreme in the sphere of " All-India " interests, which transcended the outlook as well as the function of the local authorities.

The second principle was in its way even more notable ; it was not, like the first, a reversion to a sounder political integration ; it was something entirely new. For the first time a sphere of authority was demarcated for which the ultimate responsibility would vest, not in the British Parliament, but in provincial councils based upon an Indian electorate. The provincial executives were divided into two portions. One, which retained Law and Order, Finance, Security Services, and other vital powers, remained as before, a link in the old administrative chain, stretching from the provincial government through the Government of India to Parliament. But the other, which was given Health, Education, Local Self-government and other "nation-building" departments, was made responsible to the provincial legislature. Thus the theory of the absolute responsibility of the Indian administration, from its highest to its lowest branches, to Parliament, was irretrievably breached. But at the centre, where the subjects in which the educated classes were most interested—Defence, National Finance, and the like—were handled, the executive remained irremovable ; although the Legislature became bicameral ; was largely augmented in numbers and prestige by a heavy non-official majority ; and was given extensive powers both of initiation and of obstruction.

The complication of the constitution lent much importance to the personal element. At first it seemed to work reasonably well. Congress and Mr. Gandhi, now committed to "complete independence," and the awakening of the masses to a consciousness of the political wrongs they suffered through alien rule, held aloof ; and the new legislatures were filled by the old moderate elements. The British administrators, with the disciplined loyalty characteristic of them, accepted the new régime, and tried to work it to the best of their capacity, although many disagreed with it. In some Provinces, the distinction between the two halves of the executive was blurred, and something like a joint Cabinet was constituted. In others, where the distinction was maintained, a certain friction was experienced. It was noticeable that the constitution seemed to function most easily where there was a religious or social bond to keep the majority-party in the legislatures together; in the Punjab, where the Muslims were in a majority; in Madras, where a non-Brahmin (entitled " Justice ") party emerged from the Hindus and acquired power. Everywhere the strain upon the British officials was considerable. Moreover, they lacked parliamentary training; and were often at a disadvantage as compared with the practised speakers on the Opposition benches. It was remarkable, on the whole, how successfully they defended the policy of the executive.

But the position gradually became more difficult. The moderate element in the legislatures, partly from conviction, partly from a desire to show that they were no less patriotic than the Left, were perpetually urging new demands. Refusals, the interposition of the Governor-General's discretionary powers, and consequent friction with the executive, combined at once to alienate them from the new constitution and to weaken their prestige in the country. Before long the legislatures were captured by Congress—now convinced that they provided a useful arena for staging obstruction and mass demonstrations.

Mr. Gandhi, though subject to recurrent periods of

political eclipse or quiescence, pursued a campaign of social, economic, and religious regeneration, admirable in itself, but producing political repercussions that added much to the difficulties of the executive. Among his many remarkable achievements must be accounted his awakening of the conscience of the Hindu community to the age-old wrongs of the depressed classes ; and his deliberate guidance of the mind of the student community from the morasses of anarchic crime to the idealism of benevolence and non-violence. India owes him a deep debt of gratitude for these ; while his anxiety to ameliorate the lot of the masses, his insistence on the old Hindu ideals of piety and simplicity, and his unaffected friendliness even to political opponents, have profoundly influenced the whole character of the nationalist movement. He must also be credited with a large share in the political awakening of educated Indian women. As we have noticed, the traditions of India are opposed to female education, and while Western learning was making great headway among the male members of the literate classes, progress among women was slow. Even in 1931, out of a British Indian female population of 123 million only $1\frac{1}{4}$ million were literate in any language ; and only about 150,000 were literate in English. But from about 1917 (when a deputation of Indian women approached Mr. Montagu with a request for enfranchisement) there has been a definite feminist movement in India, and its sympathies have been predominantly in the direction of Home Rule. A special section of the Congress party was organized for women by Mr. Gandhi, and they took a prominent (and to Government embarrassing) part in the mass-movements of the Left.

About this time another factor emerged to complicate

the Indian political position. One unforeseen consequence of the part played by India in the war was the acquisition of a semi-international status. Indian representatives participated in the War Cabinet, signed the Treaty of Versailles, were present in their own right at successive Imperial Conferences. India itself was an original member of the League of Nations, a member of the Governing Body of the International Labour Organization, and was recognized as among the eight leading industrial countries of the world. Indian internal affairs thus became of interest to a wider public than that of Britain ; and the attention attracted by Mr. Gandhi, due to the picturesque nature of his activities, and his personal idealism, became a distinct factor in the relationship between Britain and certain other countries—notably America. British parliamentary and public opinion was again stirred to action. The more precise status assigned to the Dominions and the recognition of their equality with Britain made it desirable to examine India's position more closely, particularly in view of the political tension then existing. Accordingly the Commission which was to examine the working of the new régime in India was dispatched earlier than had been intended.

The opinion of educated India felt itself affronted that the Commission was purely parliamentary in composition, and Sir John Simon and his colleagues were boycotted. Before their very valuable survey could be published, an effort was made by Lord Irwin (Viceroy 1926–31, now Lord Halifax) to arrange a kind of armistice with Mr. Gandhi and Congress ; and a declaration was published recognizing Dominion status as the goal of British policy in India. A new method of considering

India's constitutional problem was evolved—that of a Round Table Conference between British and Indian statesmen.

This method was partly designed to conciliate the natural desire of Indian political leaders to assist in framing schemes for the future government of their country, and partly to meet a problem now emerging in crucial form—what was to be the position of the Indian states?

In earlier chapters we have already noticed that more than one-third of India has remained organized in political units under Indian rulers; and we have seen that similar units have played a notable part in all India's political integrations. In the process of acquiring domination in India, the British entered into engagements and treaties of various kinds with these Hindu and Muslim kingdoms, controlling their external relations, but leaving them in various degrees internally autonomous. In the half-century that followed the Mutiny, when British India was being linked together by the policy of centralization, the Indian states perforce remained isolated, and for the most part materially undeveloped. They were proud—as they are to-day—of their traditional sovereignty and of their relationship with the British Crown, by whom they are recognized as trusted allies. They had no particular liking for the educated classes in British India; but since they were autonomous in their own governments, they were not hostile to British Indian aspirations so long as these were confined to British India. Before long the gradual increase of British Indian influence over the policy of the British administration, consequent upon the development of the legislatures, began to disturb the rulers of the states. More and more the activities of the centralized machine which controlled All-India affairs were dominated by the interests of British India, as voiced by the educated classes. To a measure of British control the states were well accustomed. But if the British administration was to be influenced by British India, should it not also be influenced by the Indian states ? How otherwise could their position be secured, and their engagements preserved ? Such questions as these soon began to perturb many Princes.

The interest manifested by the Indian states in the constitutional developments of British India is largely a creation of the present century. From the time of Lord Minto II. (Viceroy, 1905–10) leading Indian Princes were taken more and more into consultation upon such matters as the maintenance of internal security. The prestige of the states was greatly enhanced by their magnificent service during the war ; and when Mr. Montagu visited India in 1917 he found many of them keenly interested in the possibility of some political synthesis which might embrace both British India and themselves, while preserving their distinctive position. Exploratory work along these lines continued, and was stimulated both by the institution of a Princes' Chamber, which provided an opportunity for the discussion of common interests, and by the uneasy political atmosphere of British India. The Indian states in general, and certain particular Princes, became the target of attack by sections of the Left, which charged them with autocracy and with forming an alliance with British officialdom against the claims of British India.

Something must be said about both these charges. That the majority of the states were autocratically governed was true, if the existence of parliamentary institutions was the criterion adopted. But the Princes were not individual despots ; they ruled according to customary principles, well understood by their subjects, and were advised by counsellors who were generally able and experienced. In the larger states, some of which are the size of European countries, the standards of administration were high. The smaller states were less advanced ; but there was very little discontent among the people. Nor was it correct to maintain that the rulers were in any way conspiring with the British administration against " popular liberties " in British India. It was true that they stood firmly for the connection with Britain, and that they disliked disorder ; and were to that extent in sympathy with the efforts of the British to restrain it. But for the rest, they were patriotic Indians, and looked eagerly enough for India's advance towards a higher status within the Commonwealth. Moreover, they had their own differences with the Government of India, which in their view seemed sometimes to ignore their treaty-guarded interests in deference both to administrative convenience and to the alleged demands of All-India economic and political requirements.

The states accordingly took measures to remind the public of Great Britain that they were an element to be reckoned with in any future constitutional adjustments. They were disappointed at the results of an inquiry into their position by a Committee presided over by the late Sir Harcourt Butler ; but they succeeded in their main endeavour of securing a share in the shaping of the new Indian constitution. Since the Princes and their peoples were not, legally speaking, British subjects, the plan of procedure by way of a Round Table Conference was inevitable if they were to be integrated with the rest of India.

The proceedings of the three sessions of the Round Table Conference illustrated in remarkable degree both the sectionalism of the Indian peoples and their traditional impulse towards co-ordination. The number of interests represented was very large—at the second session Mr. Gandhi himself was induced to present the Congress point of view. But, for the most part, Congress, although the most powerful organization in India, held aloof. The tasks which lay before the Conference might well have appeared unsurmountable. Conflicting interests had to be reconciled ; the apprehensions of the Muslims and other minority communities had to be allayed; the requirements of external and internal security had to be reconciled with the claims of constitutional advance ; a balance had to be struck between centripetal and centrifugal forces ; a plan had to be found which could embrace in a common whole British India and the Indian states. But the joint statesmanship of Britain and India at length evolved the complex compromise eventually, after infinite difficulties and protracted consideration, embodied in the Government of India Act of 1935.

On the three main principles underlying the new constitution there was a remarkable measure of agreement. These were Federation, Responsibility at the Centre, Autonomy in the units. On the degree to which expression should be given to these principles there was infinite divergence of opinion, and the eventual result has satisfied no one. The states were, and are, concerned at the sacrifice of sovereignty which the new political integration will require of them ; although the majority of them have taken the view that these sacrifices will probably enable them to acquire a position in the All-India polity from which they can face the future with sure confidence. British Indian Hindu opinion, of the old " moderate " type, considers that the states have been assigned too large a share in the central machinery ; that they may prove an anti-democratic element ; that the " safeguards " and restrictions designed to ensure stability still leave far too much discretionary authority to the British ; and that although the provincial constitutions are reasonably liberal, there is very little room for true parliamentary responsibility in the Centre, where the executive, at least in times of crisis, is very powerful. The Muslims are suspicious of the Central arrangements, in which they fear Hindu domination, particularly disliking the presence of the states, whose rulers are for the most part Hindus. The Muslims have consolidated their power in four provinces as a result of the first elections ; and the Muslim League is now a powerful, consciously militant, body supported by almost every section of the community in its determination to keep Hindu power within bounds. The other minority communities are on the whole dissatisfied with the arrangements made to protect their interests, and, like the Muslims, dread the prospect of Hindu domination. The British administrators regard the whole plan as very complicated ; and although they are doing their best to make it a success, there is some uneasiness at the thought of so much power falling into untried hands.

During the interval which elapsed between the Round Table Conference and the passing of the Government of India Act in 1935, the political situation in India became very strained. Congress " declared war " on the administration, and was for a period proscribed as an illegal body. Lord Willingdon (Viceroy, 1931–36) handled the situation with tact and strength, and a calmer atmosphere gradually prevailed. But, as might have been expected, the Congress party from the first opposed the new constitution, mainly on the grounds that it has been imposed on India by the British. There is now a large section among the younger men, led by Mr. Jawaharlal Nehru, an ex-President of Congress, whose opposition is directed against the " capitalistic " character of this or any other polity which does not base itself upon economic communalism. Nevertheless, under the influence—still as great as ever—of Mr. Gandhi, the Congress organization was persuaded to contest the first elections, with the result that it obtained a working majority in seven provinces, and has staffed the provincial Cabinets. There its experience has led it to form a higher opinion of the British officials, who have loyally executed the orders of new political superiors who but lately were their bitterest opponents. On the whole, despite some trouble early this year over the release of political prisoners, the provincial Cabinets have exercised their authority with moderation, and the difficulties have nowhere proved insuperable, thanks to growing goodwill on either side. The position of the new ministers is not easy. They have given many pledges to their electorate—an electorate increasingly clamant for far-reaching changes. They are also embarrassed by the activities of their own Left Wing, which resents their firm insistence upon law and order. But they have embarked upon an energetic programme of education, both primary and secondary, with emphasis upon handicraft and vocational training. They are devoting much attention to village uplift ;

to the difficult relations between landlords and tenants. Broadly speaking, they deserve much credit for what they are doing ; they are completely in earnest and are working desperately hard.

Congress is still officially committed to the goal of " complete independence " ; and has announced its fixed hostility to the federal centre, as envisaged by the Act of 1935, on the grounds that there is no real " responsibility " there, and that the inclusion of the Indian states is a device for perpetuating the dominance of Britain. But the situation is hopeful ; there is no hostility to the ideal of federation as such, and the success of the provincial governments may shortly check the growth of the Socialist anti-Imperial party.

The complicated negotiations necessary to secure the accession of the Indian states—who cannot be hurried— will shortly be in train ; and when once the arrangements for instituting the federal centre have been completed, the Congress may decide—as it decided in the case of the provinces—to embark upon the new venture without prejudice to the ideals of non-co-operation.

It would seem prudent to hasten slowly in the completion of the constitution ; and to rely upon the influence of reflection rather than upon compulsion. There seems little danger that the provinces will in the last resort decline to participate in the formation of a federal centre ; although the process may take longer than was at first conjectured. We may take comfort from the lessons of history.

The profound political instinct which has always insisted upon the necessity of a central co-ordinating force to restrain the centrifugal tendencies of the local units is not likely to fail at this juncture, unless it should be once again frustrated by violence and chaos.

As to the extent to which the arrangements set forth in the 1935 Act will require modification in the light of experience it is impossible to prophesy. But that the principles upon which the Act is based are not only inherently sound, but in harmony with the requirements of India as exemplified time after time in the history of the country, I trust no reader who has followed this narrative thus far will remain in doubt. Given external peace and internal order—both of which are safeguarded so far as is compatible with provision for the vesting of real power in the Indian people—Britain may hope that India's advance towards true self-government will proceed steadily and surely. But these two requirements are essential ; for the weakest, because the newest, element in India's political equipment is the conception of a national government, competent, within its sphere, to control All-India matters. It would not take very extensive or very protracted internal disorder to resolve India once more into a congeries of local units ; while, if the lessons of history are to be trusted, a successful invasion consequent upon the breakdown or withdrawal of effective British protection would have this result almost immediately.

That the constitution of India under British domination should, throughout the last hundred years, have tended almost unfalteringly towards the parliamentary type of democratic government is a most remarkable phenomenon, in view of the peculiar difficulties presented by local conditions. If India should succeed in the present endeavour to enter the comity of democratic countries, this event must mark a turning-point not merely in the history of the British Commonwealth, but also in the development of the governmental systems of mankind.

CHAPTER VIII

THE ECONOMIC BACKGROUND OF INDIA

Is it true that India was once a wealthy country which has been exploited and victimized by British rule ? And is it true that Britain has killed Indian industries ? We may perhaps preface our survey of economic conditions by a brief examination of these charges, which are often made, even to-day, and are confidently repeated by many persons who have no opportunity of knowing the true facts.

From what we have already learned of India's history, it seems unlikely, on the face of it, that any country so afflicted by external invasion and internal disorder could ever have been wealthy as wealth is understood in Western countries ; and any careful examination of historical sources shows that this impression is correct. India's trade with the West, which has existed at least since pre-Roman times, has been based upon the fact that the country produces certain commodities which were highly prized in Europe. Since these commodities had to be paid for in bullion—Europe then produced little that India would buy in exchange—India became known from early times as " the grave of the precious metals " ; and it was assumed that a country which absorbed so much gold and silver must necessarily be wealthy. But the precious metals were in fact sterilized by being used for personal adornment and for ceremonial purposes ; no system of banking could make headway against the hoarding habit. Thus they fell a ready prey to plundering invaders, of whom India has known so many, and the country derived little benefit.

·The European travellers who visited India during the heyday of the Mughal Empire—among the best and most highly organized Imperial systems India ever knew before the coming of the British—have left records which show that while the nobility possessed hoards of jewels and bullion, the mass of the people existed in miserable poverty. Then, as now, the vast bulk of the population dwelt in villages and lived by agriculture. Despite the more merciful ratio—one-sixth of the gross produce—prescribed by the Hindu law books, the commonest share taken by the state was from one-third to one-half. The peasants had to be forced, by brutal cruelties practised from time to time, to cultivate the land, and would, when they found it possible, " run away to the Rajas "—the small feudatory kingdoms— to escape the severities of the Imperial revenue-collectors. Predial slavery was general ; the labourers were bound to the soil. There was no incentive to save even when saving was possible, for the Imperial Exchequer claimed all the personal property of those who died possessed of anything.

Famines of terrible extent are recorded, when whole provinces perished of starvation, when cannibalism was practised and " a child's body was more esteemed than his love." Moreover, owing to the self-contained nature of the village economy and the absence of good roads, there was little scope for industrial production. The only industry developed on any extensive scale was hand-spinning and weaving. The fine muslins, chintzes, silks, and cottons which Europe prized so highly were luxury articles, produced to meet the demand of the various courts, imperial and local, up and down the country ; and the artisans themselves, as Bernier reported to Colbert, were most miserably paid and harshly treated.

Such was the economic organization of the greater part of India when the East India Company began its commercial career. The Company was, of course, little interested in agriculture until it became itself one of the " country Powers " ; but it was extremely interested in industrial production. It was confronted by a number of difficulties ; first, the impossibility of any considerable trading except for cash ; secondly, the manifold obstacles—in the shape of tolls, transit duties, bandits, and bad roads—to internal trade ; and thirdly, the very ill-organized sources of supply of the goods it wanted. But by degrees a working system was evolved ; and the Company afforded an increasing stimulus to Indian trade by the wealth it poured into the country. The second point is worth stressing. In 1674, for example, the Company spent £85,000 in Bengal alone in purchases of silk, taffeta, and saltpetre. By 1680, the figure had risen to £150,000 ; next year it was £230,000.

Moreover, through its steady purchase of goods for export, a regular organization was built up. In various parts of the country subordinate factories were founded, with local branches for particular districts. In each local branch the Company employed Indian contractors, through whom arrangements for the supply of fabrics were made with weavers, and money advanced for the materials—the common practice of the country. Difficulties sometimes arose on both sides, for the weavers often failed to discharge their contracts, and the Indian agents of the Company were prone to abuse their authority. The Company passed frequent regulations to prevent the ill-treatment of the weavers ; but the necessity of guarding against fraud made it inevitable that the work should be supervised. Hence arose a number of complaints, some only too well founded, which have received great prominence in the works of those who attack the record of the British in India.

It should in fairness be remembered that the English merchants did much to keep Indian industries alive during the anarchy of the eighteenth century. When the Mughal power declined, the Company stepped into the breach, gave employment to artisans, and provided a market, which would otherwise have been entirely lacking, for their products. The Company's trading activities also helped to draw different parts of the country into economic unity, and thus prepared the way for future developments. The weakness of the system was twofold ; first, that it was modelled upon contemporary Indian practice, and was accordingly by no means free from an element of exploitation ; and secondly, that the industries themselves were artificial, in the sense that they had no widespread local demand to support them, but were organized as luxury trades for export or for the small class of nobility. They thus never became firmly rooted, and could withstand no competition.

The accusation that the Company destroyed indigenous industry is thus the very contrary of the real facts ; it made its living by the encouragement of the export trade. But it met great opposition from vested interests in England ; and early in the eighteenth century Parliament prohibited the wearing of certain classes of silks, calicos, and muslins. The Company's trade in these goods, so far from falling off, increased ; for a large market was developed on the Continent. Within the next three-quarters of a century, however, two events occurred which did severely affect Indian industry ; but neither of these could be laid to the door of the Company. The first was the recurrent hostilities between Britain and France, which from time to time closed the Continental market ; the second was the invention of spinning and weaving by power.

Some writers have sought to maintain that the Industrial Revolution in England was founded on the plunder of Bengal ; but this is disproved by chronology alone. The first steam spinning-mill was not at work in England until 1785—more than a quarter of a century after Plassey—and it was not until the next few years that the export of English cotton goods rose appreciably. When this occurred, Indian handicraft industry could not compete. In 1793 it was said in London "that every shop offers British muslins equal in appearance and of even more elegant patterns than the Indian at one-fourth less in price."

Doubtless in its own interests, the Company did what it could to save the situation. It made great efforts to improve the quality and extend the cultivation of Indian cotton, for which England provided a ready market. It also did its best to foster the silk industry of India ; importing Italian and French experts to improve on crude local methods, and inducing Parliament, early in the nineteenth century, to give a tariff preference of 20 per cent. to Indian silk. These endeavours were not very successful, for the Indian workmen as a whole did not take kindly to the new methods. But there is no reliable evidence that compulsion was ever practised ; and such artisans as would consent to work in the Company's " model factories " received greatly enhanced wages.

A beginning was made in jute production and the foundation of the present-day industry was laid. Indigo factories were started, and although here abuses later crept in through the victimisation of labour by private individuals in outlying districts, the trade brought no small wealth into the country. By the early years of the nineteenth century, over £1½ million was said to be paid each year for rent of land and hire of labour. The Company also endeavoured to encourage Indian ship-building, aided by abundant supplies of teak. But manu-factured iron was prohibitively expensive in India ; too little iron in their construction had made Indian ships in the old days unsuitable for heavy weather ; and the new attempt to compete with British shipyards was a failure.

From 1813 onward the Company, as we have seen in an earlier chapter, lost its monopoly of Indian trade, and the entry of British private commercial enterprise and private capital commenced. There seemed little prospect of applying either to the spinning and weaving or to the silk industry. The new-comers, therefore, turned their attention to the dual task of increasing the country's exports of commodities and enlarging, in return, the market for British goods. For the next quarter of a century there was not much progress in either direction ; for internal commerce was still hampered by the many local dues which the British had inherited from the Mughals, or which they had not been able to persuade the Indian states to abolish ; while the high tariff walls by which Britain protected her own interests, real or supposed, prevented the growth of any large export trade. But a great change came in the middle of the last century, with the florescence of the Free Trade era. British capital flowed to India in increasing quantities, and found its best opportunity, not in industries—for iron, steel, and coal were not readily to be had—but in railway development, irrigation schemes, and other projects connected with India's major enterprise—agriculture.

The subsequent stages in this development we shall shortly trace ; but it is clear that the worst charge which can be levelled against the early economic policy of the British is that they did not anticipate the modern idea of fostering industries, which had first to be created, by a high tariff wall erected at the expense of the consumers.

In fact, the accusation that the British have ruined India does not accord with the available evidence. The population of India has increased steadily under British rule, so that to-day the country is supporting far more people, and, as we shall see, supporting them rather better, than at any period of which history tells. Since the first census of the Indian Empire (including Burma) was taken in 1872, the nominal increase has been no less than 144 millions ; and when allowance is made for the inclusion of additional areas and for the more scientific methods of enumeration characteristic of later reckonings, the real increase stands at just under 88 millions. During the ten years preceding the last census, taken in 1931, the increase was 34 millions (only 6 millions less than the entire population of France) bringing the total up to 353 millions. It is estimated that in 1941 the population of the Indian Empire and Burma will be in the neighbourhood of 400,000,000. The density of the population worked out in 1931 at 196 per square mile ; but this average is of little significance, since a large part of the total area is desert country or mountainous regions. In detail, the density varies from as little as 6.5 per square mile in Baluchistan to 4,000 per square mile in certain parts of the south-west coast. Largely owing to the social customs of the people, which prescribe the married state as essential, and insist upon entrance thereon almost immediately after puberty, the birth-rate is extremely high : 35.5 as compared with 16.1 in England and Wales. But the death-rate, explicable principally on climatic as well as social grounds, is high also : 25.9 as compared with 11.6 for our country ; and the average expectation of life is only twenty-five years, as compared with fifty-eight years with us.

The great mass of this population—313 millions at the last census—lives in rural areas. In a country as large as Europe without Russia there are only thirty-eight towns which have more than 100,000 inhabitants ; and the urban population is only 11 per cent. of the total—an increase of less than 1 per cent. over the ratio in 1921. Thus, while the large industrial and semi-industrial towns show signs of benefiting at the expense of the smaller towns, the urban population is doing little more than hold its own with the rural. Nearly 70 per cent. of the population live by agriculture and husbandry ; while something like 90 per cent. dwell either in villages or in quite small towns.

From the days when the Company became a territorial power in India, the British have always been greatly concerned with the welfare of the rural masses. It is true that they have been criticised, particularly by Nationalists, for not doing more ; but it is very doubtful whether the full extent of their work has ever been appreciated. We have seen the efforts made by Warren Hastings to protect the peasantry, and to ensure that they enjoyed the fruit of their toil ; and the traditions he established have guided generation after generation of British administrators who have found their life-work in rural India.

The land-system in India is extremely complicated, and those readers who desire to follow its details are referred to the many technical treatises which exist. But its economic importance is such that some of its characteristics must be briefly described. By immemorial tradition, it has always been the duty of the peasant to cultivate the land, and to pay a share of the gross—which has varied from time to time—to the state. In the old Hindu law books the share was prescribed as one-sixth of the gross ; but under Muslim rule—particularly under the Mughal Empire—the ordinary share was between one-third and one-half. The state share was in practice taken in one of two ways : either by negotiation direct with the village as an administrative unit, or by " farming out " the estimated value to an intermediary who guaranteed a fixed sum and got what he could over and above this from the cultivators.

Both these systems the British inherited. In Bengal, where they had their first experience of revenue administration, they found that the state share was being collected by a number of intermediaries, who paid in theory nine-tenths of the collections to the state, retaining the tenth part for their trouble. But in practice they had long paid fixed sums. In an endeavour to stabilize the position these sums were, after some experiments, " settled " in perpetuity; so that the revenue-" farmers " became in effect landlords subject only to the payment of a quit-rent to the state. This is the so-called " Permanent Settlement of Bengal," which is often adversely criticized on the ground that the landlords absorb all the benefits of agricultural improvements. Elsewhere in India, where the " farming " of revenue prevailed, the " farmers " were confirmed in their position, but subject to a variation in the quit-rent, which was based upon what the tenants actually paid. The quit-rents are revised from time to time, generally at twenty or thirty year intervals. Where there was no intermediary to be found, the British, like their predecessors, dealt directly with the villages, and also in many cases with the individual villagers ; and here also the rates are revised at regular intervals.

But the British have been faced with a complication which never troubled the Mughals. In the old days there was more land than there were peasants to cultivate it. With the institution of British peace and order, and the consequent increase of the population, the position became reversed. There was great competition for land, and landlords could make terms which left little more than a bare subsistence to the tenants. The British have intervened with an elaborate system of Tenancy Acts, limiting the enhancement of the dues and securing tenants from eviction. Broadly speaking, the present-day position is that in rather more than half of the total area paying land-revenue, the system of settling state dues directly with the villager prevails ; about one-third is in the hands of landlords subject to periodic assessment ; and about one-fifth is permanently settled.

It has been calculated that the total share of the produce paid by the peasant averages 5 per cent. of the gross, and rarely exceeds 10 per cent. Even so, there are complaints that the incidence of the land revenue is too heavy. During recent years, when falling prices of agricultural produce in the world-market have adversely affected the cultivator, he has shown signs of interesting himself in " No Rent " campaigns and other demonstrations organized by Congress workers against both the landlords and the Government. There is a growing disposition to complain of the dues taken by the landlord, who is in some parts of India often an absentee, and in general does not fulfil many of the obligations, such as supplying capital and maintaining buildings, which are expected from him in the West. " No Rent " campaigns at the present moment are a source of some embarrassment to Congress ministers—now responsible, under the new Constitution, for law and order in the provinces—who were formerly active in promoting them. But the whole question is receiving careful attention. That additional flexibility is needed in the fixation of new rates may be true. It is significant that a few years ago, when political agitation induced the Government of Bombay to re-examine the new rates suggested for the Bardoli district, it was found on inquiry that the new assessment was too high. It is clear, none the less, that the British rates leave the peasant, whether he deals directly with the state, or deals through a landlord, a larger margin in hand than has hitherto been the case. And it may be added that there is no evidence that there is any general decline in the fertility of the soil ; although the extension of cultivation to inferior soils may have reduced the average productivity to some extent.

One of the most striking features of British rule in India has been the immense development of irrigation. The dependence of agriculture on rainfall, and the disastrous effects of the failure of the monsoon, have been recognized by successive Indian administrations from a very remote date ; and the East India Company found many old works, varying in size and importance from considerable canals to tiny storage tanks, in various parts of the country. A large number of them were in ruins ; and in no case did they make the most scientific use of the resources available. The Company at first confined its efforts to repairing and extending these works, finding the cost out of revenue. It then began projects of its own ; and also allowed private enterprise—not very successfully—to participate. When the Crown assumed the governance of India, irrigation works were greatly extended, for large loans raised in England were applied to their construction.

By degrees, a highly-organized system was evolved, which has brought millions of acres of land, much of which lies outside the area of rainfall altogether, under cultivation. Some of the works are highly profitable ; others have been undertaken, not because they can pay their way, but because they afford protection to regions where rainfall is very scanty. Further, Government has given much encouragement by financial aid to the old Indian practice of well and tank irrigation, which now provides for as much as one-third of the total irrigated area of India.

But the most startling record is that of canal construction. The total length of main and branch canals and distributaries is now about 75,000 miles—by far the largest system in the world—irrigating an area of 33 million acres. Every year the value of the crops on land irrigated by Government works is greater than the entire capital outlay on the works themselves. This capital outlay up to 1918 amounted to no less than £74 million ; and since that time projects costing another £49 million have been undertaken and are nearing completion. It is probable that eventually more than 50 million acres will be irrigated from canals alone. Several of the Indian states, such as Bahawalpur, Patiala, and Bikaner, have extensive canal systems of their own ; and the last mentioned has the longest concrete-lined canal in the world.

The original object underlying all the irrigation works has been to lay the spectre of famine, with which India is always menaced owing to the irregularity of the monsoon rainfall. Indian history recalls frightful famines, in which cannibalism was practised, and whole tracts of country went out of cultivation for years because all the inhabitants had perished or had fled. This is now mercifully forgotten, for the British have evolved an elaborate machinery to deal with the whole matter. Quite apart from the influence of irrigation, which now releases millions of acres of land from the vagaries of rainfall, full advantage has been taken of the fact that the monsoon never fails simultaneously in every part of India. Improved means of communication now enable grain to be sent where it is wanted ; weekly reports keep the Government informed of the progress of the crops in every part of India ; and every province has prepared a programme of useful work ready to be undertaken, on which the agriculturists whose crops have failed may find employment. Payment is made by the state ; and those who cannot work are fed also. Relief is financed by a Famine Insurance Fund instituted in 1876, and the fund further enables loans to be made to distressed cultivators for the purchase of ploughing cattle, seed, and implements.

Much useful work has been done by the Central and

Provincial Departments of Agriculture to improve the quality of seed available to the Indian farmer, and to introduce improvements in the methods of cultivation. Mistakes have been made ; for the agriculturalist, with the tradition of centuries behind him, is skilled in his own business, and in the early days sometimes confounded the Western-trained experts. But the work of the trained advisers—now for the most part young and enthusiastic Indians—has been more adapted to Indian needs and is steadily increasing in importance. Improved varieties of seed have put large profits into the hands of the cultivators ; and constant research work is being pursued to isolate strains which experience has shown are well suited to the country. The crops which are of the greatest commercial importance are rice, wheat, cotton, and sugar ; and on all of them much directly-profitable work has been done. Continuous efforts are also being made to improve the breed of draught and milch cattle, although religious traditions make this work exceptionally difficult in India.

Among the most useful of the things which the British have done for the masses in India, apart from the supreme service of peace and order, is the improvement in the system of internal and external communications. In its 42,000 miles of railways India has a very fine property, representing an investment of almost £650 million. The state owns seven-eighths of the capital, three-quarters of the mileage, and directly manages about half the total length of line. Nearly 650 million passengers are carried annually, and nearly 90 million tons of goods.

Road development has also been considerable, though it is still inadequate ; and since the advent of the motor car and the motor bus, road transport is playing an increasing part in linking together villages and towns. There are now about 270,000 miles of roads; and the facilities offered by motor transport have caused an increasing demand for their extension. One of the most characteristic sights of India to-day is the village omnibus, crammed to bursting-point inside, with additional passengers sitting on the roof, clinging to the mud-guards, and even to the radiator. A special petrol cess now provides funds to improve the surface of the roads and extend them to outlying areas. It must further be noticed that the Indian Posts and Telegraphs Department has taken an important share in promoting communications by carrying 1,400 million postal articles every year, and by controlling 450,000 miles of telegraph wire. Telephonic development is slow, except in large centres; but trunk lines are multiplying.

We have already had occasion to notice some of the political consequences of the improvement of communications, and have seen how the educated classes have been drawn together into a new unity. But the economic consequences have been at least as important; we have seen that in time of dearth, grain can be sent to famine-stricken areas from districts where the crops are good; and this exemplifies the fact that the resources of the whole country can for the first time in its history be to some extent co-ordinated. Before the introduction of railways and roads, every village in India lived an isolated life. Crops could only be disposed of in the local market; " harvest gluts " were normal happenings; and while, when the crops failed, the people died, a succession of good years would ruin even prosperous farmers, who could obtain nothing for their produce. This state of affairs has now largely passed away, for the Indian farmer has been brought into touch with the world-markets by railways and roads. There are still large numbers of very isolated villages, which are cut off from neighbouring centres of population, especially during the rains ; but it is fair to say that the country is being more closely knitted into a single economic unit with every year that passes.

The economic consequences of opening up the country by better internal communications have been enhanced by the development of cheap and speedy sea transport. Following on the opening of the Suez Canal, India's agricultural products—cotton, jute, oilseeds, rice, wheat, tea, and many other commodities—found ready access to the world-market, with the result that a great and growing export trade has been built up. Between the years 1851 and 1936 the value of this trade rose from £18 million to just under £130 million. The development has been primarily due to the fact that the world's ability to utilize tropical agricultural produce greatly increased in the latter half of the nineteenth century ; and India was thus able to secure a market for its produce just at the time when the increasing population provided a new demand for certain classes of European goods.

Industrial development lagged behind, partly because (as we have seen) there were no industries which offered attractions to British investors comparable with those which arose in connection with agriculture ; and partly because India's mineral resources are limited and have not proved, until recently, at all easy to develop. More-over, the expansion of India's overseas trade coincided with the great Free-Trade era of Britain ; and it was impossible for India to compete with Britain in manufactured goods without the shelter of a protective tariff —which to the orthodox economist in those days would have been regarded as almost an unholy thing, and entirely contrary to the principles of " the wealth of nations."

Indian Nationalists still complain of what they regard as the unfair treatment which India received during this period ; and have never forgotten that in 1894, when the tariff on imported cotton goods was raised by $3\frac{1}{2}$ per cent. to increase the revenue of the Government of India, pressure from Lancashire manufacturing interests forced the Government to impose an equivalent excise duty on Indian mill-made cloth. It is also asserted that the whole lay-out of the Indian railway system has been deliberately designed to encourage the exploitation of India's raw materials for the benefit of British manufacturers, and to enable British goods to penetrate in every quarter and thereby to damage indigenous industries.

Regarding the first charge, there is no valid defence. The action was in accordance with the canons of political economy then fashionable ; but was only taken against the protests of the Government of India because Lancashire pressed for it. It was a piece of selfishness for which a high price has been paid in subsequent ill-will and suspicion. Of the second charge it must be said that the source of British power in India has always been the sea, and that it was inevitable that easy access to and from the ports should be the principal object of early railway policy. But it may be noted that in the recent progress of Indian industries—so marked since the last war—the location of the railways has been found well adapted to the requirements of the country.

For a good many years prior to the time when, in

1919, India acquired control over its own tariff, without interference from the Home Government, educated Indian opinion had been pressing for a policy of protection which, it was claimed, would assist industrial development. Originally, no doubt, the desire for industrial development sprang from increased middle-class unemployment ; for Western education was producing young men unfitted for agricultural pursuits far in excess of the absorption capacity of Government service or the learned professions. But the instinct behind the demand was sound ; India's economy had become too narrowly based, since it rested so largely upon agriculture. There were, it is true, important industries like the jute industry, which had been developed by British capital ; but there were few enterprises—the Bombay and Ahmedabad cotton mills were notable exceptions—which were under Indian direction.

This state of affairs is now being altered, and modern power industries are growing steadily. A policy of " discriminating protection," intended avowedly to build up indigenous industries, is administered by a Tariff Board. Some progress has been made. The great Tata Iron and Steel Company pointed the way to promising developments ; and there have been many successful companies launched under Indian direction and with Indian capital, which has only recently been willing to participate in industrial enterprises. Also the number of Indian shareholders in British companies is increasing. Whether industrial development in India can, within a reasonable period, proceed far enough to affect in any appreciable way the economic position of the masses, still remains to be seen. But educated Indian opinion is determined to press ahead ; and has now fortunately the power to do so. The proportion of manufactured to non-manufactured goods in India's export trade slowly increases ; but there are great handicaps, prominent among them being the dearth of skilled labour, and the migratory character of the Indian factory-hand, who is in essence a rustic anxious to return to his village when he has made a little money.

What is the general economic condition of India to-day ? It must be stated frankly that the widespread poverty of the Indian people impresses all observers. The great majority of Indians live in a way which would be quite impossible in a more rigorous climate ; and their appearance strikes the observer as pitiably poor, depressed, and melancholy. We have already seen that the British have made great efforts to improve their lot. Nevertheless, the total result, if judged by the present condition of the masses, still leaves much to be desired. Why is this ?

One cause, no doubt, is the great increase in the population. India is still at the stage when the people seem to multiply to the very limit of their resources ; so that improved standards of life only result very slowly from improved economic conditions. There is certainly very great pressure upon the cultivable land ; and it has been calculated that when the land used for growing produce for foreign markets is subtracted from the total area, India has to feed, and to some extent clothe, its population from what about two-thirds of an acre per head can produce. Also, there is much fragmentation of holdings, due to the universal desire for land ; and actual division has proceeded in many parts to an extent which is quite uneconomic. The result is that there are more people on the land than the land can support in any degree of comfort ; and a large class of landless labourers, whose livelihood is seasonal and precarious, has grown up.

Yet the Indian villager enjoys many advantages denied to the poorer classes in Western countries. The climate simplifies the problem of clothes ; except for certain parts of the country at certain times of the year, anything more than a loin-cloth is an embarrassment to the manual worker. For almost all the year fuel is scarcely needed for warmth, and it is only in the towns and largest villages that shelter costs anything. The villager builds his house himself out of materials that lie ready to hand, generally sun-baked bricks and thatch. He does not make much use of artificial lighting, for he both rises and rests at an early hour, and the annual variation of the hours of sunlight is small in comparison with that in the British Isles. His tools and appliances are very simple, and he needs little gear of any kind in his home. He grows practically all his own food, and his necessary purchases are very small indeed.

The truth seems to be that one fundamental cause of the poverty of the Indian masses is to be found in the fact that they are not organized socially for the production of wealth. We have already noticed the typically "other-worldly" outlook characteristic of much of India, and this outlook, as we have seen, is reflected in the social structure. There is little incentive to individual advancement ; and the community spirit discourages initiative and makes for traditional ways. The general consequences of this situation must be noticed, for they are cumulatively of great importance.

Unlike the Western peasant, the Indian cultivator has little of the close frugality that grudges no sacrifice to improve the land. He has small working capital ; and does not much labour to accumulate it when accumulation is possible. He prefers to maintain a low standard of living at the cost of little exertion, rather than to increase his resources by greater effort. His average production is thus very low ; and the fact that in many parts of India he need do little more than scratch the soil and scatter seed, encourages him to be content to live, rather than to strive to live well. Further, although the climate compels him to remain idle for something like one-third of the working days of the year, he does not take up subsidiary industries, like sericulture, pig-keeping, fruit-growing, and poultry-farming. Here the influence of the caste system enters ; for such pursuits are confined to separate groups and do not fall within the province of the ordinary farmer. Again, while the Indian agriculturalist does not accumulate capital for the improvement of the land, he is compelled by social custom to much wasteful expenditure for marriages and festivals. A year's income will thus be spent in a few days ; and the peasant is often heavily and hopelessly in debt to the moneylender. The security which he enjoys under the tenancy legislation has not been an unmixed blessing, for it permits him to mortgage his land up to the hilt.

Something has been done of late to tackle the problem of rural indebtedness by the encouragement of the co-operative movement ; and the state of Bhavnagar has made a notably courageous effort to effect a drastic cure by buying up the debts owed to moneylenders and allowing the debtors to compound on easy terms. But so radical a solution has not been found possible in British India, where the problem is so enormously greater ; and

debt remains among the main causes of the Indian cultivator's poverty.

Finally, religious and social practices often hinder him
from making the best use of such resources as he has.
The seclusion of women is not generally practised among
the labouring classes except by Muslims ; but the pre-
valence of infant marriage, of various disabilities which
women suffer by tradition, and of dysgienic social conditions, have serious effects upon the health, as well as on
the material productivity, of an entire half of the population.

The Indian peasant, in fact, is alike hampered and
supported at every turn by his traditional conservatism.
He uses butter very wastefully, and will not utilize the
cheap and abundant coco-nut oil, which is eagerly
purchased by the wealthy countries of the West. He
maintains large quantities of useless cattle, which he
may not destroy even though they consume far more
than they produce. It has been calculated that the
annual loss involved by the existence of such cattle
amounts to four times the entire land revenue of the
country. Bone meal he may not use, and bones, hides,
horns, and skins he may not touch. His abhorrence of
taking life in any form exposes him to ruinous depredations from monkeys and rats. Rats alone cost India
about £50 million a year—more than military defence.
In past ages he has ruined forests for firewood ; and
now to-day, despite the progress which has been made
in reafforestation under the Government's direction, he
must burn much animal manure—which should go back
to the land—for cooking fuel.

Such a state of affairs is not susceptible of any sudden
or dramatic change, yet until it is improved India will

almost certainly remain poor because the *per capita* productivity of the population is so small. The enormous numbers of people involved, their poverty, their ignorance, their lack of all initiative, their insistence upon traditional ways and ancient shibboleths—all combine to make real progress towards economic advancement very difficult. Something can be done, and is being done, through the co-operative movement, through the spread of education, through "village uplift," to alter the attitude of the masses towards economic advancement. Mr. Gandhi's encouragement of hand-spinning has been useful, as affording employment at seasons of the year when time would otherwise be wasted ; and the introduction of subsidiary industries of various kinds would be among the most directly hopeful lines of advance. Mr. Gandhi is interesting himself actively in this also ; and is endeavouring to remove the prejudice against employing bone meal, utilizing hides and skins, and making good economic use of dead animals. He is also encouraging training in craftsmanship ; and hopes to make the village less dependent upon mechanical civilization and more reliant upon its own resources.

In the towns, where congestion is very bad and the worker, in chronic indebtedness to the moneylender, often lives under conditions of intolerable squalor, welfare work among the labouring classes is increasingly engaging the attention of the Government, of the municipalities, of private employers, and of Indian and British philanthropists, both men and women. But progress is slow, for the industrial worker is still a villager at heart, and all his habits are fundamentally unsuited to the social and sanitary requirements of urban life. It is also against his inclination to assert individualistic claims ; and he can with difficulty be induced to take advantage of the excellent labour legislation which now exists, and is elaborated almost yearly. Not much is to be expected immediately from Trade Unionism, which is a comparatively recent growth, and still to some extent dominated by political considerations in which the economic interests of the workers, and their education in the task of protecting their rights, do not always enjoy priority.

Are the Indian masses becoming poorer or richer under British rule ? To the careful observer there is considerable evidence, both direct and indirect, in favour of the latter alternative. The annual railway returns show that the travel habit is growing. Statistics of imports show that sugar, paraffin, cotton piece-goods, boots and shoes, matches, soap, which were once used only by the wealthy and middle classes, are now being increasingly purchased by the labouring classes. The house of the average villager is better than that in which his father lived ; and he often eats better food. He uses brass vessels where his father used coarse earthenware. He no longer gives his wife brass bangles as a matter of course. Often they are now of silver. He smokes manufactured cigarettes. Perhaps most significant of all, the consumption of cotton piece-goods, now mainly of Indian manufacture, has increased 35 per cent. per head of population.

The change has not, of course, been all to the good ; for the contact now made with the world markets, while it has brought profit, has also brought risk. A slump in world-prices now causes distress to many. Of recent years the Indian farmer has had cause to thank the conservatism which has prevented him from devoting his energies entirely to profitable non-food crops. He has kept to the old plan of growing enough food for himself ;

so that even when the price of silver falls and his wife's bangles—often the only form of reserve—are reduced in value, he does not wholly lack food. It is this spirit which Mr. Gandhi desires to strengthen and encourage, in order to stop any " drift " to the towns and to restore India's ancient village economy.

Figures of average income are of little value as a guide to the economic position of the Indian masses ; for even at the present time the villager does not live in a monetary economy ; he gets many things in kind instead of in cash ; and, as we have noticed, enjoys other things at little or no cost. But for what these estimates are worth, they show an increase. About 1880 it was calculated that the average *per capita* monetary income was about 27 rupees. In 1901 this worked out at 30 rupees. By 1911 it was about 50 rupees. In 1921 very careful estimates made by the Statistical Branch of the Madras Department of Agriculture showed that the average for that part of India was about 100 rupees. The broad accuracy of this figure was borne out by parallel investigations in Bombay. Making allowance for the prices then obtaining, the real increase during the preceding twenty years was about 10 rupees. So that even if movement is discouragingly slow, it is at least in the right direction.

Is it true that India is ground down by the exactions of a too-costly Government ? As against the average income already noticed, the average incidence of taxation is about 6 rupees per annum. The actual demand of the state on the land works out in most places to about 5 per cent. of the gross produce—a figure which may be compared with the corresponding average of 17 per cent. in Japan. English civil servants and police officers number about 1,300 ; there are only 3,500 British in all the higher grades of all the services taken together ; and out of the total of 1½ million Government employees—not a large number to look after the civil administration and public services of 350 million people—there are only 12,000 British from top to bottom, including many in quite subordinate positions. Thus, despite high salaries, the administration of India is one of the cheapest in the world, measured by the burden on the people. It is to be regretted that out of total public revenues of about £140 million, central and provincial, about £34 million has to be spent upon defence ; but, as our study of Indian history has shown us, security is the basis of everything, and without it no progress at all is possible. Even so, taking the great nations of the world, India has the lowest *per capita* defence expenditure ; for it works out only to about three shillings and sixpence per head.

Stress is sometimes laid by Nationalist critics upon the sterling remissions to England, which have been called "Drain," "Tribute," and other opprobrious names. But almost all the money remitted is interest on loans borrowed at very low rates—far lower than India could have obtained except on British credit—and employed for productive purposes. Of the total interest-bearing obligations of the Government of India, amounting to less than £900 million in India and Britain combined, over £700 million is covered by interest-yielding assets, the profits of which not only cover interest charges on the original loans, but also afford a substantial revenue to the state. Deadweight debt, amounting to about £130 million, is exceptionally small, and a testimony to the careful administration of public finance.

The system of public finance is too complicated for

exposition in a book of this brevity ; its outlines have from time to time corresponded with the administrative decentralization we have already traced. At first, the Government of India held the purse-strings and made doles to the provinces. With the Montagu-Chelmsford Reforms the position was reversed, and the provinces were expected to assist the Centre. The abolition of the " provincial contributions" was a great step towards popular control over provincial finance ; which in the new Federal constitution is governed by an elaborate division of revenue-heads between the Centre and the Units. Every one is agreed that large revenues are required to enable the autonomous provinces to improve the condition of the masses, but no one seems quite clear how the money is to be found. That something must be done to increase India's very small public revenues is obvious. In this direction also there is progress, but it is slow in comparison with the urgent needs of the country. Already the old entire dependence of the Budget upon the land revenue has been modified, and Customs and Income Tax, Forests, and Railways are of increasing importance. Perhaps the ingenuity of the Indian Ministers of Finance will succeed in solving this baffling problem. It is encouraging to notice that the gloomy prognostications of those who feared that India was too poor to pay the cost of the new governmental system are in a fair way to be falsified. The ministers in the provinces are showing themselves both capable and courageous in their budgetary planning.

It is on this note of hope that we may conclude our brief survey of the problems presented by India's connection with the British Commonwealth. Our own generation is not responsible for the creation of this

connection ; present-day statesmanship has already resulted in its modification in certain fundamentals. If it
were in our power to rewrite the history of our dealings
with the peoples of India, there are no doubt some
passages which we should desire to alter ; some—these
much rarer—which we would fain erase completely.
But whatever criticisms may be made, and whatsoever
their justice, concerning British rule in India, this at least
is abundantly clear : British rule, alone among the many
dominions India has known in its tragic history, has
placed the country on the road which leads alike to
national integration and to national self-government.

SUGGESTIONS FOR FURTHER READING

THE literature relating to India is inexhaustible, and I can only mention books which I have myself found particularly useful or notably interesting.

GENERAL

The best brief survey of Indian conditions is that of the Statutory Commission (Cmd. 3,568 of 1930), volume i. This may be supplemented by the two compact symposia entitled *Modern India* and *Political India*, edited for the Oxford University Press by Sir John Cumming. The *Indian Year Book*, published by *The Times of India* (last edition, 1937–38), is a mine of statistical and general information.

HISTORICAL

There is no one-volume History of India as good as the importance of the subject demands. *The Oxford History of India* is excellent for facts, and it is easy to find one's way about ; but its general outlook is rather depressing. *The Cambridge Shorter History of India* is better written, but much more difficult to refer to, and contains no devices—such as variations of type—to lighten its somewhat lengthy paragraphs. Of more elaborate works, *The Cambridge History of India* is indispensable to the serious student. Multi-volumed, and the work of specialists, its function is to be consulted rather than to be read. Its bibliographies are admirable.

But there are two volumes—unfortunately both rather large and expensive—which between them cover most of the ground. Rawlinson's *India : A Short Cultural History ;* and Thompson and Garratt's *Rise and Fulfilment of British Rule in India.* For the British period, P. E. Roberts's *History of British India* is good, and is also compact. My *History of India—British Period*—was written for Indian undergraduates, and thus assumes a certain amount of knowledge ; but is necessarily small and inexpensive. For constitu-

tional history there is the admirable work of Dr. Berriedale Keith :
A Constitutional History of British India, which is both learned and
provocative. The 1935 Act is fully described in Sir Shafa'at Ahmad
Khan's *The Indian Federation*. Lord Zetland describes events leading
to the Act in *Steps towards Indian Home Rule*.

FICTION

One of the pleasantest ways of learning something of India is to
read a few of the admirable novels dealing with the country. For
the days of Rajput chivalry, Forrest's *Ruby of Rajasthan* and Irvine's
The Devil's Finger may be commended. Meadows Taylor's *Con-
fessions of a Thug* is deservedly famous. There are so many novels
dealing with the Mutiny that it would be invidious to attempt a
selection ; anyway, it is an unhappy episode. For modern India,
there is a wealth of choice. Kipling's *Kim* is among the great novels
of the world. Edmund Candler's *Abdication* and *Sri Ram, Revolutionary* are unequalled in their way. Forster's *A Passage to India* it
would be an impertinence for me to praise. Thompson's *An Indian
Day* and *Farewell to India* I have found delightful ; and the same
author has just published a novel dealing with the life of Buddha.
In *Torteval* and his collection of short stories Hilton Brown (" H.B."
of *Punch*) describes life in southern India. Two charming novels
by Indians are *The Brothers*, by Tagore, and *Athawar House*, by
Nagaranjan. Louis Bromfield has shown in *The Rains Came* that a
novel on India can be a best-seller.

REMINISCENCES

For those who do not care for fiction, but have not the time for
lengthy study, there are numerous Memoirs. For the early days of
British rule, *The Memoirs of William Hickey* may be commended.
Sleeman's *Rambles and Recollections of an Indian Official* is admirable
for pre-Mutiny days. Our own times have proved very rich in
first-class work. Sir Walter Lawrence's *The India we Served* is most
attractive in its mellow wisdom. Francis Yeats-Brown's *Bengal
Lancer* is famous. Sir Michael O'Dwyer's *India as I knew it* describes
the lifework of a brilliant administrator. Irvine's *Land of No
Regrets* (1938) is first-class. Other notable books are Edwin Montagu's *An Indian Diary* ; Banerjea's *A Nation in the Making* ; Lady
Minto's *India, Minto and Morley* ; M. K. Gandhi's *My Experiments
with Truth* and other autobiographical works ; and the autobiog-

raphy of J. L. Nehru. There are also numerous reminiscences by soldiers, among these Roberts's *Forty-one Years in India* is notable.

READING SUPPLEMENTARY TO THE CHAPTERS

Chapter I

Rapson, *Ancient India*; Heimann, *Indian and Western Philosophy*; Senart, *Caste in India*; Banerjea, *Public Administration in Ancient India*; Jayaswal, *Hindu Polity*; Mukerjee, *Democracies of the East*; Arnold, *The Caliphate*.

Chapter II

Callender, *The Naval Side of British History*; *Census of India*, 1931, volume i; Slater, *The Dravidian Element in Indian Culture*; V. Smith, *Early History of India*.

Chapter III

Vincent, *Defence of India*; Davies, *The Problem of the North-West Frontier*; O'Malley, *The Indian Civil Service*; Durand, *The Making of a Frontier*; Curry, *The Indian Police*.

Chapter IV

Wheeler, *Early Records of British India*; Anderson, *The English in Western India*; Cultru, *Dupleix*; Forrest, *Life of Clive*; Monckton-Jones, *Warren Hastings in Bengal*; Malcolm, *Political History of India*; Bute, *Private Journals of the Marquis of Hastings*; Cunningham, *History of the Sikhs*.

Chapter V

Greig, *Life of Sir Thomas Munro*; Boulger, *Life of Lord William Bentinck*; Ilbert, *Government of India*; Thompson, *Metcalfe*; Holmes, *History of the Indian Mutiny*; Mayhew, *The Education of India*.

Chapters VI and VII

Ronaldshay, *The Heart of Aryavarta* ; Lovett, *History of the Indian Nationalist Movement* ; Besant, *India, Bond or Free ?* and *How India Wrought for Freedom* ; Mayhew, *Christianity and the Government of India* ; Matthews, *The Clash of Colour* ; Gedge and Choksi, *Women in Modern India* ; Shyam Kumari Nehru, *Our Cause* ; Panikkar, *Indian States and the Government of India* ; Haksar and Panikkar, *Federal India* ; Coatman, *Years of Destiny* ; Panikkar, *The Maharaja of Bikaner* ; Anon., *The British Crown and the Indian States* (published by P. S. King). Lee Warner, *Protected Princes of India : Report of the Indian States Committee* (Cmd. 3,302 of 1929).

Chapter VIII

Hamilton, *Trade Relations between England and India* ; Pillai, *Economic Conditions in India* ; Anstey, *The Economic Development of India* ; Jack, *The Economic Life of a Bengal District* ; Darling, *The Punjab Peasant* and *Rusticus Loquitur* ; Brayne, *Village Uplift in India.* For criticism of British policy see Lajpat Rai, *Unhappy India* ; Reynolds, *The White Sahibs in India* ; Dadabhai Naoroji, *The Poverty of India* ; R. C. Dutt, *Economic History of India* ; Subhas Bose, *The Indian Struggle.*

INDEX

INDEX

PRINTED IN GREAT BRITAIN AT
THE PRESS OF THE PUBLISHERS